EMERALD

GUIDE TO HOUSING LAW

Roger Sproston BA MSc

Emerald
www.emeraldpublishing.co.uk

Emerald Guides
Brighton BN2 4EG

© Straightforward Publishing 2008

British Cataloguing in Publication data. A catalogue record is
available for this book from the British Library.

ISBN 9781847160 87 4

Printed in the United Kingdom by GN Press Essex

Cover Design by Bookworks Islington

CONTENTS

1. UNDERSTANDING THE LAW   5

2. THE PROTECTED TENANT   11

3. SECURE TENANTS   20

4. ASSURED TENANCIES   41

5. JOINT TENANCIES   48

6. MOBILE HOMES   49

7. AGRICULTURAL TENANCIES   52

8. RENT AND OTHER CHARGES   67

9. THE RIGHT TO QUIET ENJOYMENT   74

10. REPAIRS AND IMPROVEMENTS   77

11. THE LAW AND OWNER OCCUPIERS   84

12. OBLIGATIONS OF FREEHOLDER/LEASEHOLDER   92

13. OWNER OCCUPIERS AND SERVICE CHARGES   110

14. ENFRANCHISEMENT AND EXTENSION OF LEASES   124

INDEX

Introduction

This Second Edition of Guide to Housing Law is a wide-ranging book dealing with all aspects of the law as it governs the relationship between people and the ownership and tenancy of land.

The relationship between landlord and tenant has always been complex and has changed immeasurably over the centuries, particularly in the 20th century, with the huge social changes that have transformed the structure of the ownership of land. Gradually, the law has provided more and more protection for the tenant, eroding the privileges of the main land owning classes.

This brief book covers the main areas of housing law and all of the requisite Acts. The general nature of tenancies is covered, along with the main obligations of landlord and tenant. Repairing obligations and assignments are covered in depth.

One new area of law that is included is the Housing and Regeneration Act 2008. The provisions of this Act will come into force gradually by the introduction of commencement orders. References to the Act are made in various parts of the text.

The other main Housing Acts are covered in depth along with business tenancies and agricultural tenancies. So too is the law concerning service charges and also extension of leases and purchase of freeholds.

Although no book covering housing law can be totally comprehensive, as the subject area is vast, this particular book attempts to cover the main areas that both the layperson and the student of law need to know.

Roger Sproston 2008

1

UNDERSTANDING THE LAW

Explaining the law

In order to fully understand the law we should begin by looking at the main types of relationship between people and their homes.

The freehold and the lease

In law, there are two main types of ownership and occupation of property. These are: freehold and leasehold. These arrangements are very old indeed.

Freehold

If a person owns their property outright (usually with a mortgage) then they are a freeholder. The only claims to ownership over and above their own might be those of the building society or the bank, which lent them the money to buy the place. They will re-possess the property if the mortgage payments are not kept up with.

In certain situations though, the local authority (council) for an area can affect a person's right to do what they please with their home even if they are a freeholder. This will occur when planning powers are exercised, for example, in order to prevent the carrying out of alterations without consent.

Leasehold

If a person lives in a property owned by someone else and has a written agreement allowing them to occupy the flat or house for a period of time i.e., giving them permission to live in that property, then they will, in the main, have a lease and either be a leaseholder or a tenant of a landlord.

The main principle of a lease is that a person has been given permission by someone else to live in his or her property for a period of time. The person giving permission could be either the freeholder or another leaseholder.

The position of the tenant

The tenant will usually have an agreement for a shorter period of time than the typical leaseholder. Whereas the leaseholder will, for example, have an agreement for ninety-nine years, the tenant will have an agreement, which either runs from week to week or month to month (periodic tenancy) or is for a fixed term, for example, six-months or one-year.

These arrangements are the most common types of agreement between the private landlord and tenant.

The agreement itself will state whether it is a fixed term or periodic tenancy. If an agreement has not been issued it will be assumed to be a fixed term tenancy.

Both periodic and fixed term tenants will usually pay a sum of rent regularly to a landlord in return for permission to live in the property (more about rent and service charges later)

The tenancy agreement

The tenancy agreement is the usual arrangement under which one person will live in a property owned by another. Before a tenant moves into a property he/she will have to sign a tenancy agreement drawn up by a landlord or landlord's agent. *A tenancy agreement is a contract between landlord and tenant.*

The contract

Typically, any tenancy agreement will show the name and address of the landlord and will state the names of the tenant(s). The type of tenancy agreement that is signed should be clearly indicated. This could be, for example, a Rent Act protected tenancy, an assured tenancy or an assured shorthold tenancy. In the main, in the private sector, the agreement will be an assured shorthold.

Date of commencement of tenancy and rent payable

The date the tenancy began and the duration (fixed term or periodic) plus the amount of rent payable should be clearly shown, along with who is responsible for any other charges, such as water rates, council tax etc, and a description of the property you are living in.

In addition to the rent that must be paid there should be a clear indication of when a rent increase can be expected. This information is sometimes shown in other conditions of tenancy, which should be given to the tenant when they move into their home.

The conditions of tenancy will set out landlords and tenants rights and obligations.

Services provided under the tenancy and service of notice

If services are provided, i.e., if a service charge is payable, this should be indicated in the agreement. The tenancy agreement should indicate clearly the address to which notices on the landlord can be served by the tenant, for example, because of repair problems or notice of leaving the property. The landlord has a legal requirement to indicate this.

Tenants obligations

The tenancy agreement will either be a basic document with the above information or will be more comprehensive. Either way, there will be a section beginning "the tenant agrees." Here the tenant will agree to move into the property, pay rent, use the property as an only home, not cause a nuisance to others, take responsibility for certain internal repairs, not sublet the property, i.e., create another tenancy, and various other things depending on the property.

Landlords obligations

There should also be another section "the landlord agrees". Here, the landlord is contracting with the tenant to allow quiet enjoyment of the property. The landlord's repairing responsibilities are also usually outlined.

Ending a tenancy

Finally, there should be a section entitled "ending the tenancy" which will outline the ways in which landlord and tenant can end the agreement. It is in this section that the landlord should make reference to the "grounds for possession". Grounds for possession are circumstances where the landlord will apply to court for possession of his/her property. Some of these grounds relate to what is in the tenancy, i.e., the responsibility to pay rent and to not cause a nuisance.

Other grounds do not relate to the contents of the tenancy directly, but more to the law governing that particular tenancy. The grounds for possession are very important, as they are used in any court case brought against the tenant. Unfortunately, they are not always indicated in the tenancy agreement. As they are so important they are summarized later on in this chapter.

The public sector tenancy (local authority or housing association), for example, is usually very clear and very comprehensive about the rights and obligations of landlord and tenant. Unfortunately, the private landlord often does not employ the same energy when it comes to educating and informing the tenant.

The responsibility of the landlord to provide a tenant with a rent book

If the tenant is a weekly periodic tenant the landlord must provide him/her with a rent book and commits a criminal offence if he/she does not do so. This is outlined in the Landlord and Tenant Act 1985 sections 4 - 7. Under this Act any tenant can ask in writing the name and address of the landlord. The landlord must reply within twenty-one days of asking.

As most tenancies nowadays are fixed term assured shortholds then it is not strictly necessary to provide a tenant with a rent book. However, for the purposes of efficiency, and your own records, it is always useful to have a rent book and sign it each time rent is collected or a standing order is paid.

Overcrowding and the rules governing too many people living in the property

It is important to understand, when signing a tenancy agreement, that it is not permitted to allow the premises to become overcrowded, i.e., to allow more people than was originally intended, (which is outlined in the agreement) to live in the property. If a tenant does, then the landlord can take action to evict.

Different types of tenancy agreement
We will be covering different types of agreement in depth further on in this book. The following is a brief summary.

The protected tenancy - the meaning of the term
As a basic guide, if a person is a private tenant and signed their current agreement with a landlord before 15th January 1989 then they will, in most cases, be a protected tenant with all the rights relating to protection of tenure, which are considerable. Protection is provided under the 1977 Rent Act.

In practice, there are not many protected tenancies left and the tenant will usually be signing an assured shorthold tenancy..

The assured shorthold tenancy - what it means
If the tenant entered into an agreement with a landlord after 15th January 1989 then they will, in most cases, be an assured tenant. We will discuss assured tenancies in more depth in the next chapter In brief, there are various types of assured tenancy. The assured shorthold is usually a fixed term version of the assured tenancy and enables the landlord to recover their property after six months and to vary the rent after this time.

At this point it is important to understand that the main difference between the two types of tenancy, protected and assured, is that the tenant has less rights as a tenant under the assured tenancy. For example, they will not be entitled, as is a protected tenant, to a fair rent set by a Rent Officer.

Other types of agreement
In addition to the above tenancy agreements, there are other types of agreement sometimes used in privately rented property. One of these is the company let, as we discussed in the last chapter, and

another is the license agreement. The person signing such an agreement is called a licensee.

Licenses will only apply in special circumstances where the licensee cannot be given sole occupation of his home and therefore can only stay for a short period with minimum rights.

The squatter (trespasser)

In addition to the tenant and licensee, there is one other type of occupation of property, which needs mentioning. This is squatting. It is useful for the tenant to have a basic understanding of this area of occupation.

The squatter is usually someone who has gained entry to a vacant property, either a house or a flat, without permission.

Although the squatter, a trespasser, has the protection of the law and cannot be evicted without a court order, if he or she is to be given the protection of the law, the squatted property must have been empty in the first place.

On gaining entry to a property, the squatter will normally put up a notice claiming squatter's rights, which means that they are identifying themselves as a person or group having legal protection until a court order is obtained to evict them. Even if no notice is visible, the squatter has protection and it is an offence to attempt to remove them forcibly.

The squatter has protection from eviction under the Protection from Eviction Act 1977 and is also protected from violence or harassment by the Criminal Law Act of 1977.

The trespasser who has entered an occupied property without permission has fewer rights. Usually, the police will either arrest or escort a trespasser off the premises. There is no protection from eviction. However, there is protection from violence and intimidation under the Criminal Law Act 1977.

2

THE PROTECTED TENANT

If a tenancy agreement was granted before 15th January 1989 then, in most cases, it will be a Rent Act protected agreement. However, there are a number of exceptions to this and they are listed further on in this chapter.

Many tenancies nowadays are assured tenancies. However, despite this, there are a significant number of older Rent Act protected tenancies in existence.

What Rent Act protection means is that the rules which guide the conduct of the landlord and tenant are laid down in the 1977 Rent Act.

This Act was passed to give tenants more security in their home. It is called a Rent Act because its main purpose is to regulate rents, but the Act also gives tenants other rights such as protection from eviction.

It is mainly only tenants who can enjoy protection under the Rent Act of 1977, not usually licensees or trespassers who have limited rights. A tenancy will be protected provided that the landlord does not live on the premises. If a landlord lives in the same accommodation as the tenant then the tenant will not be protected by the 1977 Rent Act. To live in the same premises means to share the same flat as the tenant and not, for example, to live in the same block of flats.

In addition, Rent Act protection means that the rent will be regulated This basically means that the tenant has the right to a fair rent set by a Rent Officer employed by the local authority.

The fair rent is set every two years and the landlord is not free to charge as he or she wishes. Once set the rent cannot be altered.

Rent Act protection also means protection from eviction which means that the landlord is not free to evict.

For a tenancy to be protected, however, the tenant must be using the property as his/her main residence. If they are not, and the fact can be proved, then they will lose protection and the landlord can evict with less trouble.

SECURITY: THE WAYS IN WHICH THE TENANT CAN LOSE HIS/HER HOME AS A PROTECTED TENANT

When a tenant signs a tenancy agreement he or she is signing a contract where both landlord and tenant are agreeing to accept certain rights and responsibilities.

In the agreement, there are a number of grounds for possession which enable the landlord to recover his or her property if the contract is broken by the tenant, eg, by not paying the rent. These may not always be referred to in the agreement but this can be found in the 1977 Rent Act.

If a landlord wishes to take back his or her property he/she must serve the tenant with a notice to quit (the premises) which must give twenty eight days notice of intention to seek possession of the property (to begin to recover the property) and, following the expiry of the twenty eight days an application must be made to court to repossess the property.

When the landlord serves the notice to quit the reasons for his doing so should be stated in a covering letter to the tenant and should be based on the grounds for possession outlined in the agreement.

A landlord cannot simply evict a tenant, or use menaces (harassment) to do so. There is protection (Protection from Eviction Act 1977) and the landlord must apply to court to get a tenant out once the twenty-eight days have expired.

When a landlord has served a notice to quit, a tenancy becomes a "statutory tenancy" which exists until a court order brings it to an end.

Briefly, the reasons for a landlord wanting possession will be based on one of ten mandatory or ten discretionary grounds for possession. Mandatory grounds for possession means that the court must give the landlord possession of the property, which means that the judge has no choice in the matter.

Discretionary grounds for possession means that the court can exercise some discretion in the matter (i.e. can decide whether or not to order eviction) and it is up to the landlord to prove that he is being reasonable. Discretionary grounds usually correspond to the tenants obligations in the tenancy.

It is very rare, in the first instance, if the grounds are discretionary, for a landlord to gain possession of a property unless it is obviously abandoned or the circumstances are so dramatic. Usually a suspended order will be granted.

A suspended order means that the tenant will be given a period of time within which to solve the problem, i.e come to an agreement with the landlord. This time period is, normally, twenty eight days. So, for example, if a tenant has broken an agreement to pay the rent, the judge may give twenty eight days in which either to pay the full amount or to reach an agreement with the landlord.

Listed below are the grounds for possession which can be used against a tenant by a landlord. Full details of all grounds can be found in the 1977 Rent Act

The discretionary grounds for possession of property covered by the 1977 Rent Act

Ground One is where the tenant has not paid his or her rent or has broken some other condition of the tenancy.

Ground One covers any other condition of the tenancy. This includes noise nuisance, unreasonable behaviour and, usually, racial or sexual harassment.

Ground Two is where the tenant is using the premises for immoral or illegal purposes, eg, selling drugs, prostitution. It also covers nuisance and annoyance to neighbours.

Grounds Three and Four are connected with deterioration of the premises as a direct result of misuse by the tenant.

Ground Five is that the landlord has arranged to sell or let the property because the tenant gave notice that he was giving up the tenancy.

Ground Six arises when the tenant has sub-let the premises, ie, has created another tenancy and is no longer the only tenant. Usually, the landlord will prohibit any sub-letting of a flat.

Ground Seven no longer exists.

Ground Eight is that the tenant was an employee of the landlord

13

and the landlord requires the property for a new employee.

Ground Nine is where the landlord needs the property for himself or certain members of his family to live in.

Ground Ten is that a tenant has charged a subtenant more than the Rent Act permits.

One other important discretionary ground does not appear in the list of grounds in the 1977 Rent Act. It relates to the provision of suitable alternative accommodation. If the landlord requires possession of the property for reasons such as carrying out building works then it must be demonstrated that suitable alternative accommodation can be provided by the landlord for the tenant.

The mandatory grounds for possession of a property occupied by a protected tenant

These are grounds on which the court must give possession of a property to the landlord. The judge has no choice in the matter. If such an order is granted then it cannot be postponed for more than fourteen days, except where it would cause exceptional hardship when the maximum is six weeks. There are two basic rules for using the mandatory grounds:

1. The landlord must give a written notice saying that he/she may in future apply for possession under the appropriate ground. He/she must give it to the tenant normally when or before the tenancy begins (before the tenancy was granted, in the case of shorthold) and;
2. When he/she needs possession, the conditions of the appropriate ground must be met.

The mandatory grounds are as follows:

Ground Eleven. This ground is available only when the landlord has served notice at the beginning of the tenancy stating when he or she wants back the premises, ie, a date is specified.

Ground Twelve is valid only when a landlord has served notice that the property may be required for personal use as a retirement home.

Ground Thirteen applies only where the letting is for a fixed term of not more than eight months and it can be proved that the property was used as a holiday letting for twelve months before the letting began.

Ground Fourteen is that the accommodation was let for a fixed term of a year or less, having been let to students by a specified educational institution or body at some time during the previous twelve months.

Ground Fifteen is that the accommodation was intended for a clergyman and has been let temporarily to an ordinary client.

Ground Sixteen is that the accommodation was occupied by a farmworker and has been let temporarily to an ordinary tenant.

PRIVATE SECTOR AGREEMENTS SIGNED BEFORE JANUARY 1989 BUT WHICH DO NOT HAVE RENT ACT PROTECTION:

Not all people who entered into agreements before 15th January 1989 will be protected tenants under the 1977 Rent Act.

The license

Private landlords have proved unwilling to accept protected tenants as it means that tenants will have the right to a low rent and will be difficult to get out. As a result, landlords have devised a number of loopholes which enable them to avoid granting a protected tenancy. One such arrangement is the license agreement.

A license is a personal arrangement between the landlord (licensor) and the licensee. The main difference between a licensee and a tenant is that the licensee, right from the beginning, has far less security than a tenant.

A license to occupy a house, or part of a house, is the same, in principle, as a license to drive a car or to run a public house. It gives permission to stay which is temporary and can be withdrawn. Landlords find licenses attractive because the protection which is given to tenants by the 1977 Rent Act and the 1988 Housing Act is not given to the licensee. This means that the landlord can evict the licensee, without giving twenty-eight days notice and without getting a court order. Or at least this seemed to be the case. Hardly surprising, then, that licenses were so popular with landlords. Courts have, until recently, looked upon licenses quite favourably as long as both parties are aware of the meaning of the agreement.

In many cases, it goes without saying, the licensee did not understand the agreement. They did not understand that the agreement was temporary and meant that they could be evicted quite easily.

However, a number of court cases in the last few years have found that an agreement seeming to be a license in fact amounted to a tenancy and therefore had protection.

In other words, the courts are taking a tougher view of landlords avoidance of protection for their tenants.

In court cases the landlord will be asked to prove that the agreement in question is in fact a license. The main difference between a license and a tenancy is quite simply that of exclusive possession. If the tenant has exclusive possession of even a room then an agreement can be held to be a tenancy and not a license.

Other agreements signed before 1989 which are not protected

There are other types of agreement which will not be classed as a protected tenancy.

Tenancies granted before 14th August 1974, and which are furnished with a resident landlord

If a tenancy was entered into before the above date and the property was furnished to a reasonable standard it is not considered to be protected. This is another complex area and will not be pursued further here.

Restricted contracts under the 1977 Rent Act

A tenancy entered into before 15th January 1989 will not be protected if, when the tenancy was first entered into, the landlord was still living in the same building as the property which has been let to the tenant. This is known as a restricted contract. The exception is the situation where the block is purpose-built and the landlord has a separate flat. However, if one landlord sells his interest to another person who intends to live in the building, the tenancy will remain unprotected for twenty-eight days. In that twenty-eight days the person taking over the property can either take up residence or serve written notice that he intends to do so within the next six months.

As long as he/she takes up residence within six months the notice serves to prevent the tenancy becoming protected.

If a tenancy is not protected because it falls within the above category then it is known as a restricted contract. However, one important point is that a restricted contract will cease to be such after the passing of The 1988 Rent Act when there is a change in the amount of rent payable under the contract other than a change determined by the rent tribunal.

From then on, the restricted contract becomes an assured tenancy. More about assured tenancies later.

Flats and houses under certain rateable values

If the property has a rateable value of over £750 (£1,500 in Greater London) that property cannot be the subject of a protected tenancy. In practice, few properties are above this figure.

Even after the change from rateable values to community charge and the council tax in 1993, the rateable value of a property will still apply in this case.

Tenancies at low rents

A tenancy which was entered into before 1st April 1990 is not a protected tenancy if the rent paid is less than two-thirds of the rateable value of the property on the appropriate day. The appropriate day is 23rd March 1973 unless the property was valued at a later date. If no rent is paid then the tenancy will not be protected.

Flats and houses let with other land

If a property is let with other land to which it is only an adjunct (an addition) then it will not be a protected tenancy. However, importantly, unless the other land consists of more than two acres of agricultural land, it will be taken as part of the dwelling house and will not prevent the tenancy being protected.

Payments for board and attendance

If a part of the rent for which a house is let is payable in respect of board or attendance there will not be a protected tenancy.

Board, which is the provision of meals, must be more than minimal if the tenancy is not to be protected. Provision of a continental breakfast would be enough, whilst the provision of hot drinks would not.

Attendance includes personal services such as making beds. This provision is one that is often used by landlords to avoid the Rent Act. Such a tenancy, though, may form a restricted contract (see above).

Lettings to students

A tenancy granted by a specified educational institution to students studying will not be protected (the institution will usually be a university or college of further education).

Holiday lettings

A tenancy is not a protected tenancy if its purpose is to give the tenant the right to occupy the dwelling for a holiday.

Agricultural holdings

A tenancy is not protected if the dwelling is part of an agricultural holding and is occupied by the person responsible for the control of the farming of the holding. Tenancies of this sort are subject to the control of the Agricultural Holdings Act 1986 and other areas of the law.

Licensed premises

Where a tenancy of a dwelling house consists of or comprises premises licensed for the sales of alcohol, there will not be a protected tenancy.

Resident landlords

The tenancy will not be protected if, at the commencement of the tenancy, the landlord was resident in the same building as the property which has been let. This does not apply if the landlord merely has another flat in a purpose-built block; he must be in the same building or residence.

Where the landlord is a local authority, the Crown, a housing association or a co-operative

The tenancy will not be protected where the landlord is one of the above. Tenants of local authorities, housing associations, the Crown or a Co-operative have a different sort of protection, which this guide does not go into.

Company lets

Only an individual person is capable of living in a flat or house. If a property is let to a company there can be no statutory (legal) tenancy. When a property is let to a company, the tenancy would be between that company and a landlord. There are certain circumstances, however, where a company let can be a protected tenancy and the fair rent legislation applies.

.3

SECURE TENANCIES

The 1980 Housing Act introduced the right to buy for public sector tenancies and also introduced a measure of protection hitherto absent. The 1985 Housing Act consolidated the 1980 Housing Act. Over the years since its inception, the 1985 Housing Act has been subject to a number of amendments, notably the 1988 Housing Act, which will be discussed later, and which shifted Housing Associations from the public sector to the private sector, but not local authorities.

Secure tenancies

The Housing Act 1985 s 79 (1) defines a secure tenancy as:

1) A tenancy under which a dwelling house is let as a separate dwelling is a secure tenancy at any time when the condition described in s 80 and 81 as the landlord condition and the tenant condition is satisfied.

There must be a tenancy of a dwelling house which is let as a separate dwelling. Unlike private sector legislation, the 1985 Housing Act does not exclude licences from statutory protection.

As far as security is concerned, a secure tenancy, as defined by the 1985 Act, will lose security if one of the conditions creating a secure tenancy is not present. We will be considering the conditions below. One of the main conditions, as we shall see, is that of maintaining the home as an only or principle home. Failure to do this, i.e. by residing elsewhere will render the tenancy non-secure. However, if at a later date, the condition becomes satisfied, i.e. the tenant moves back in then security is retained (Hussey v Camden Council 1995 27 HLR.5 CA). Where possession proceedings are brought, in deciding whether security of tenure has been lost the courts will look at the situation that existed at the expiry of the notice to quit.

The landlord condition

The main factor that defines a secure tenancy is the status of the landlord. A landlord must be one of the prescribed bodies set out in the 1985 Housing Act s 80(1). The main landlord body issuing secure tenancies is a local authority. There are other bodies which can issue secure tenancies, such as a New Town Corporation, a Housing Action Trust, an Urban Development Corporation, the Development Board for Rural Wales and, in certain cases, some housing Co-operatives.

Before January 15th 1988, Housing Associations could grant secure tenancies. After this date, they cannot and secure tenancies will only exist in Housing Associations where they have been granted pre-1988, where immediately before the granting of a new tenancy the tenant was a secure tenant of the same landlord , where a mutual exchange occurs or where a tenant is transferred as part of a large scale voluntary stock transfer from local authority to housing association.

In addition, if a tenant has been granted suitable alternative accommodation by an order of the court, and the court deems the assured tenancy to be unsuitable a secure tenancy can be granted.

In the main, the number of secure tenancies in the housing association, or Registered Social Landlord sector have dwindled and are now in a minority.

The tenant condition

The Housing Act 1985 s 81 defines tenant condition as:

a) the tenant is an individual and occupies the dwelling house as his or her only or principal home; or
b) where the tenancy is a joint tenancy and each of the joint tenants is an individual and at least one of them occupies the dwelling as his or her only or principal home.

Shared accommodation

The definition in relation to the 1985 Act is stricter than the Rent Act 1977 and the Housing Act 1988. A tenant who shares a kitchen will not be a secure tenant for the purposes of the 1985 Act. The sharing of a bathroom however, will not take the tenant outside of the Act, because a bathroom is not seen as an essential living room.

Secure licences

The Housing Act 1985 s 79(3) provides that a licensee may be a secure tenant except for licences granted to those who occupy temporary accommodation. Although section 79(3) appears to give significant protection to licensees this protection was restricted by a decision of the House of Lords in Westminster City Council v Clarke (1992) 2 AC 288. In this case it was held that a licensee could be a secure tenant only if he or she had exclusive possession of a separate dwelling house. Mr Clarke, who occupied a room in a hostel was not held to be a secure tenant. Where licensees have a secure tenancy they cannot exercise the right to buy their properties, as afforded to other secure tenants. Section 79(3) of the Act states that it is only the provisions of that part of the act that apply to licensees and not the rest of the Act, including part 5 which contain the right to buy provisions.

Introductory tenancies

An introductory tenancy is one which would have been a secure tenancy but for the housing authority choosing to adopt the introductory tenancy regime. Introductory tenancies are used by local authorities where they have decided to use this device as a sort of probation, before offering a secure tenancy. There is a trial period of one year. This device, it is hoped, will go some way to ensuring good behaviour, particularly of the worst tenants, the so called 'problem families'.

Statutory exclusions from the Housing Act 1985

Schedule 1 of the Housing Act 1985 lists the types of tenancies that cannot be secure:

- Long leases-a fixed term tenancy granted for a term-certain exceeding 21 years cannot be a secure tenancy
- Introductory tenancies-are excluded from being secure tenancies by virtue of sch 1 para 1A (inserted by the Housing Act 1996).
- Premises occupied in connection with employment-under schedule 1, para 2 of the 1985 Act, if a tenant is either an employee of the landlord or an employee of one of the public bodies listed in para 2, and the premises is occupied in connection with that employment then the tenant cannot be a secure tenant.

Even if the tenancy agreement does not specify that the tenancy is in connection with employment the court will infer that this is the case if the facts of the matter show it. If a tenant has secure status but his employment changes and the premises are seen as essential to his job then secure status will be lost. In Elvidge v Coventry Council (1993) 3 WLR 976, an employee was originally a secure tenant. He was promoted and his change in duties made it necessary the particular premises to carry out his job. The court held that he was no longer a secure tenant.

If an employee retires, this does not mean that the occupier becomes a secure tenant. Employees are excluded from protection to enable the landlord to keep control of the premises for the job.

Land acquired for development

A tenancy cannot be a secure tenancy if the dwelling house is on land which has been acquired for development and the dwelling house is used by the landlord, pending development, as temporary accommodation. This exception will apply even if the land was acquired for development by the landlords predecessor in title (Hyde Housing Association v Harrison (1991) 1 EGLR S1. However, if the development is no longer to be carried out, or in prospect, the reverse will apply (Lilleshall Housing Co-operative v Brennan (1992) 24 HLR 195).

When a person moves into an area to take up employment and accepts accommodation from a public landlord the landlord can deny secure status by virtue of sch 1 para 5 of the 1985 Housing Act. To achieve this the landlord must serve notice in writing that this exception applies. The exclusion will apply where, immediately before the grant of the tenancy the person was not resident in the area, an offer of employment was gained before the grant of the tenancy and the tenancy was granted to him/her for the purposes of meeting temporary accommodation.

If the landlord is a local housing authority the tenancy will not become secure until the housing authority has notified the tenant that it is secure. If the landlord is not a local housing authority, the tenancy will become secure after one year of grant, unless notified earlier.

Short-term arrangements

Sch 1 para 6 of the 1985 Act deals with short-term arrangements. Local authorities make arrangements with private landlords to help with finding homeless people or others, accommodation. Tenants of property sub-let from private landlords cannot therefore become secure tenants.

Other exclusions from the secure tenancy regime include:

- Temporary accommodation during works
- agricultural holdings
- licensed premises
- student lettings
- Business tenancies
- Almshouses

The terms of a secure tenancy

Although the terms of a secure tenancy are, to some extent, contractual, there are a number of terms included by statute. The Housing Act 1985 s 104 gives a public sector landlord an obligation to publish information about its secure tenancy. This will be an express term of the tenancy explaining matters such as the right to buy, right to repair, other repairing obligations etc. Section 105 of the Act places a further obligation on the landlord to consult tenants over matters of housing management.

Assigning a secure tenancy

There are certain rights to assign a secure tenancy:

- Mutual exchange
- Matrimonial or children related reasons where a court will assign
- Assignment through succession

Exchange

Section 92 of the 1985 Housing Act implies a term into every secure tenancy that the tenant, subject to fulfilling certain criteria and with landlords consent can assign a tenancy by way of exchanging the tenancy with another tenant of a local authority or housing association. The criteria relate, for example, to the size of the property, i.e. whether under or over occupation will occur and also the tenants rent account and the condition of the property.

A landlord cannot unreasonably withhold consent if the parties to the exchange fulfil the criteria.

Matrimonial proceedings

The general prohibition on assignment does not apply to property adjustment orders made under s23 and 24 of the Matrimonial Causes Act 19 under 17(1) of the Matrimonial and Family Proceedings Act 1984. Where parties divorce the courts can make an order for the transfer of tenancy from one party to another.

Assignment to a potential successor

A secure tenant may assign a tenancy during his or her lifetime provide that the person to whom he or she assigns would be qualified to succeed to the tenancy on death (Housing Act 1985 s 91 (3) C.

Sub-letting of a secure tenancy

Under the HA 1985 s93, it is a term of every secure tenancy that:

a) the tenant may allow any persons to reside as lodgers, but;

b) will not, without the written consent of the landlord part with possession of part of the dwelling.

If the tenant parts with possession of the whole of the dwelling house then security of tenure is lost and cannot be regained and a notice to quit may be served ending the tenancy. A court order must be obtained before formal ending.

If a secure tenant applies to sub-let part of the dwelling then a landlord cannot unreasonably withhold permission.

Repairs and alterations under a secure tenancy

Under the 1985 HA s 96 the Secretary of State is entitled to introduce regulations to assist tenants whose landlords are local housing authorities to have 'qualifying repairs' carried out. A qualifying repair is one which the landlord is covenanted to carry out. The regulations (Secure Tenants of local housing authorities (Right to Repair) Regulations 1994 entitle the secure tenant to apply to the landlord to have a repair carried out. The landlord should then issue a repair notice specifying the nature of the repair, the identity of the contractor and the date by which the work should be carried cut. If the repair is not carried out by this date the tenant will be entitled to compensation.

Alterations

By s 97(1) of the 1985 Act, it is an implied term of every tenancy that the tenant shall not make alterations without the permission of the landlord. Consent cannot be held unreasonably. If it is withheld unreasonably then it will be treated as consent given. If the landlord neither grants nor gives consent within a reasonable time then consent is treated as being withheld.

A tenant who has improved property may be entitled to compensation if the improvements have added to the value of the property or the rent the landlord can charge. If the improvements were made before 1st February 1994. compensation will be governed by section 100 of the housing Act 1985. These provisions were amended by s122 of the Leasehold Reform Housing and Urban Development Act 1993, so compensation for improvements begun on 1st February 1994 will be governed by s 99A and 99B which were inserted into the HA 1985 by the 1993 Act.

Variation of a secure tenancy

Secure tenancy terms can be varied in three ways:

a) by agreement with the landlord and tenant
b) in accordance with the provisions of the tenancy agreement
c) in accordance with s 103 of the 1985 Act

Terms which have been implied by statute cannot be varied. Section 103 only applies to a secure periodic tenancy. It sets out the procedure to be followed by a landlord who wishes to vary a secure tenancy. This is achieved by notices governed by timescales.

Rent

The Housing Act 1985 contains no system of rent control, in contrast to the 1977 Rent Act. Local Authorities are entitled by section 24(1) of the 1985 Act to 'make such reasonable charges as they may determine for the tenancy or occupation'.

Security of tenure under the 1985 Act

The Housing Act 1985 restricts only the landlord's rights to end a secure tenancy. A tenant can still terminate a tenancy by use of a notice to quit. The tenancy will contain the process within which the tenant should give notice.

The landlord has to follow a strict process in order to determine a secure tenancy. If the tenancy is fixed term, the landlord will wait until the term has expired before taking possession. If the tenant does not vacate then a court order must be obtained, on one of the grounds for possession listed further on.

Periodic tenancies

Most secure tenancies are periodic tenancies. This cannot be brought to an end by service of a notice to quit. The landlord has to follow a set of procedures laid out in the 1985 Act s 83 and 83A.

Proceedings for possession can only be started if a notice of seeking possession, in accordance with s 83, has been served on the tenant. The main principle when serving notice is that the tenant has to receive the notice. This is known as 'proof of service'. The court may consider dispensing with a notice of seeking possession if it is just and equitable to do so. The notice of seeking possession must state the date after which court proceeding will begin, an application for possession applied for. Generally speaking, this is after 28 days but it is custom and practice to apply after the rent date (Monday) after the 28th day has expired. The notice remains in force for 12 months days after expiry. Proceedings cannot be brought under a notice after this time and a new notice must be served.

S83(2) provides that a notice seeking possession must:

a) be in a form prescribed by regulations made by the Secretary of State
b) specify the ground on which the court will be asked to make an order for possession of the dwelling house
c) give particulars of the ground

The information must be sufficient and clear enough for the tenant to understand and to remedy the breach of agreement.

The court cannot make an order for possession on a ground for possession unless it is stated in the notice, but the landlord may be ale to alter or add grounds with leave of the court.

If the landlord is attempting to recover possession under ground 2, for nuisance or other anti-social behaviour then a slightly different notice is required. This notice must state that proceedings for possession may be begun immediately and also specify the date sought by the landlord as the date by which the tenant must give up possession. The reason for the difference is that if a landlord is taking action for anti-social behaviour then the landlord may have to act quickly depending on the severity of the behaviour. See grounds for possession.

Succeeding to a secure tenancy

The Housing Act 1985 s 87 provides that a person is qualified to succeed to a secure tenancy if he or she occupies the dwelling as an only or principal home at the time of the tenants death and is either the tenants spouse or is a member of the tenants family and has resided at the property for a period of 12 months prior to death.

A tenants spouse will be entitled to succeed provide that he or she was occupying the marital home as principal home when the tenant died. A spouse means a married partner although a fairly recent decision in Ghaidan v Godan Mendoza (2003) 2 WLR 478 makes it seem likely that same sex couples living together must be treated equally to avoid discrimination under Article 14 of the European Convention for the Protection of Human Rights. The recent Civil Partnerships Act 2004 will also have a bearing on this.

A member of the tenant's family must fulfil the residence requirement of 12 months, i.e. living in the home for 12 months prior to death before succession is granted. Section 113 defines a member of the family as a spouse, a person who lives with the tenant as man and wife, parent, grandparent, child, grandchild, brother, sister, uncle, aunt, nephew and niece. It also provides that half blood relationships are to be regarded as whole blood, i.e. stepchildren and illegitimate children treated as legitimate. A de-facto spouse will be counted as a member of the family and has to fulfil the 12-month residence requirement.

The residence requirement for family members does not demand that the person living with the tenant lived in the property to which that person is seeking to succeed. For example, in Waltham Forest Council v Thomas (1992) 2 AC 198, two brothers lived together for more than two and a half years and then moved to a new house. It was found that one brother was entitled to succeed to the secure tenancy when the other brother died 10 days after the move.

The Housing Act 1985 permits only one succession. If the deceased tenant was already a successor, no one will be able to succeed to the tenancy. A person who has become a sole tenant of a joint tenancy will be treated as a successor. Where a joint tenant becomes a sole tenant following death the remaining tenant will be deemed to be a successor.

If a tenant who is a successor is granted a new tenancy of the same dwelling house within six months of the end of the previous tenancy, that person will not be regarded as a successor.

If more than one person is entitled to succeed to a periodic secure tenancy, it is the spouse who will take precedence. If the deceased person had no spouse and has two or more family members entitled to succeed the family must decide amongst them. If no agreement can be reached the landlord will decide.

Where there is no person qualified to succeed, the tenancy will be disposed of either in the will of the tenant or to the intestacy rules. If this is the case the tenancy will cease to be a secure tenancy unless the vesting or disposal of the tenancy is in pursuance of an order made under s23 or 24 of the Matrimonial Causes Act 1974. Once a tenancy ceases to be secure security cannot be regained.

If the tenancy is for a fixed term it will be disposed of under a will or intestacy. The same rules as above apply.

Other provisions for secure tenants

Part V of the housing Act 1985 extends the right to buy to secure tenants. This enables tenants to buy their properties at a discount from local authority landlords. The Housing and Regeneration Act 2008 will introduce changes to the RTB regime for secure tenants.

Part V of the 1985 HA confers upon the secure tenant the right to buy either the freehold or to be granted a long lease of the dwelling house in which he or she is resident. A lease will normally be for 125 years with a low ground rent, typically £10.

The right to buy can belong to only a secure tenant or to a person closely connected to a secure tenant, for example, a family member. If the secure tenancy is a joint tenancy, the right to buy belongs jointly to all of the tenants or to one of them as may be agreed. Where there is only one secure tenant, that tenant may choose to share the right to buy with not more than three members of his or her family regardless of the fact that the family members are not joint tenants. To be eligible to share the right to buy a family member must be a tenant's spouse, a family member who has been residing with the tenant for 12 months previously or a family member to whom the landlord has consented to the right to buy.

Tenants must satisfy a qualifying period as a resident which is currently five years (after July 2005. The qualifying period does not have to be with one landlord but can be with any number of social landlords.

Excluded properties from the right to buy

The Housing Act 1985 s 120 provides that the right to buy will not arise in the cases specified in sch 5 to the Act. The most important exceptions are as follows:

a) the landlord is a charitable housing trust or association
b) the landlord is a co-operative housing association
c) the landlord is a housing association which has never received a grant of public funds
d) the landlord does not own the freehold or an interest sufficient to grant a lease 21 years in the case of a house or 50 years for a flat
e) where the dwelling house forms part of a building which is held mainly for purposes other than housing and was let to the tenant in consequence of the tenants employment by the landlord.
f) where the dwelling house was designed or altered to make it suitable for occupation by physically disabled persons
g) where the dwelling house is one of a group of dwelling houses which it is the practice of the landlord to let for occupation by persons who suffer a mental disorder and social services and special facilities are provided
h) Where the dwelling house is one of a group of dwelling houses particularly suitable for elderly persons and special facilities are provided.

Section 21 provides also that the right to buy cannot be exercised where a court order is in effect and the tenant is obliged to give up possession of the dwelling house or the person, or one of the persons who have the right to buy is an undischarged bankrupt or has a bankruptcy provision pending against them or has made a composition or an arrangement with his or her creditors the terms of which remain unfulfilled.

The preserved right to buy

Tenants will retain their right to buy in the event of a large scale voluntary transfer of housing stock from a local authority to a housing association, or other body set up to take the transfer. Section 171 (b) of the 1985 guarantees the right to buy, known a the preserved right to buy with certain modifications as long as the tenant continues to occupy the property a their only or principal home.

Procedure for the right to buy

A strict notice-driven procedure is in place for the exercise of the right to buy. The tenant will apply initially using an RTB1 form. The initial application can be withdrawn at any time up to completion.

If after notice has been given and there is a change of tenant the new tenant will be treated as if he or she had given the notice. This is relevant to circumstances such as succession or other legitimate assignment. The new tenant will also be eligible for the discount claimed in the notice by the former tenant. Likewise, if there is a new landlord the new landlord is placed in the position that the old one was in.

Once a notice has been served the landlord will have four weeks to reply or eight in the case of having to apply to different landlords for a reference to fulfil the residency criteria. Within this period the landlord will either admit or deny the right to buy.

Using form RTB2.

Following the issue of the RTB2 the landlord will, if the RTB has been admitted, serve a s125 notice stating details of purchase price, original valuation and discount and also the costs of major repairs and decorations over the next five years. This is an important

32

notice, tying the landlord in to a fixed service charge in respect of major repairs The landlord has eight weeks to produce this notice of freehold and twelve weeks if leasehold.

The tenant can dispute the valuation carried out by valuers instructed by the landlord and can appeal to the district valuer whose findings are final.

The tenant must serve a further notice on the landlord within twelve weeks of receiving the s125 notice. The notice must state whether or not the tenant intends to pursue the RTB or whether to withdraw the claim. If a notice is received but the tenant still does not pursue the claim the landlord will serve a prior notice to complete which gives the tenant 56 days to complete. If this period elapses then the landlord will serve a final notice which gives the tenant 56 days to complete. After this final period the landlord will withdraws the offer.

The price payable for the property in question will be the open market valuation less discount. The amount of discount has changed. In London for example, where the discounts used to be in line with the rest of the country, it is now a flat £16,000. In addition, if a tenant sells their property within five years then a proportion f the discount, gradually reducing, is repayable.

The Right to Acquire for tenants of registered social landlords

In order to overcome the problem of those people who do not qualify for the right to buy, i.e. the vast majority of housing Association Tenants on assured tenancies, the government introduced the right to acquire for tenants of registered social landlords. This was introduced by the Housing Act 1996. Tenants who have occupied housing association property for two years or more, on a secure or assured tenancy, will have the right to buy if their property was built with public funds or substantially refurbished with public funds after April 1997. There are some exceptions to the right to acquire, such as properties in rural areas and properties which have been specially adapted.

The 1985 Act Grounds for Possession of a secure tenancy

As with all tenancies, if there is a breach of agreement, the landlord will need to take action to end that agreement. In the case of secure tenancies there are 17 grounds for possession which the landlord can rely on.

1.   Grounds for possession

Grounds 1 - 8: Grounds on which the Court may order possession if it considers it reasonable

Ground 1: Rent arrears or other breach of tenancy

Rent lawfully due from the tenant has not been paid or an obligation of the tenancy has been broken or not performed.

Ground 2: Nuisance

The tenant or a person residing in or visiting the dwelling-house-

■   has been guilty of conduct causing or likely to cause a nuisance or annoyance to a person residing, visiting or otherwise engaging in a lawful activity in the locality, or

■   has been convicted of-using the dwelling-house or allowing it to be used for immoral or illegal purposes, or an arrestable offence committed in, or in the locality of, the dwelling house.

Ground 2A: Domestic Violence

The dwelling-house was occupied (whether alone or with other) by a married couple or a couple living together as husband and wife and –

■   one or both of the partners is a tenant of the dwelling-house, one partner has left because of violence or threats of violence by the other towards that partner, or a member of the family of that partner who was residing with that partner immediately before the partner left, and the court is satisfied that the partner who has left is unlikely to return.

Ground 3: Waste and neglect

The condition of the dwelling-house or of any of the common parts has deteriorated owing to acts of waste by, or neglect or default of, the tenant or a person residing in the dwelling-house and, in the case of an act of waste by, or neglect or default of, a person lodging with the tenant or a sub-tenant of his the tenant has not taken such steps as he ought reasonably to have taken for the removal of the lodger or sub-tenant.

Ground 4: Damage to furniture
The condition of furniture provided by the landlord for use under the tenancy, or for use in the common parts, has deteriorated owing to ill-treatment by the tenant or a person residing in the dwelling-house and, in the case of ill-treatment by a person lodging with the tenant or a sub-tenant of his, the tenant has not taken such steps as he ought reasonably to have taken for the removal of the lodger or sub-tenant.

Ground 5: Misrepresentation
The tenant is the person, or one of the persons. to whom the tenancy was granted and the landlord was induced to grant the tenancy by a false statement made knowingly or recklessly by-

- the tenant, or
- a person acting at the tenant's instigation

Ground 6: Premium on assignment
The tenancy was assigned to the tenant, or a predecessor in title of his who is a member of his family and is residing in the dwelling-house, by an assignment made by virtue of section 92 (assignments by way of exchange) and a premium was paid either in connection with that assignment or the assignment which the tenant or predecessor himself made by virtue of that section.

In this paragraph 'premium' means any fine or other like sum and any pecuniary consideration in addition to rent.

Ground 7: Misconduct in tied accommodation
The dwelling-house forms part of, or is within the curtilage of, a building which, or so much of it as is held by the landlord, is held mainly for purposes other than housing purposes and consists mainly of accommodation other than housing accommodation, and-

- the dwelling-house was let to the tenant or a predecessor in title of his in consequence of the tenant or predecessor being in the employment of the landlord, or of a local authority, a new town corporation , a housing action trust an urban development corporation the Development Board for Rural Wales, or the governors of an aided school, and

- the tenant or a person residing in the dwelling-house has been guilty of conduct such that, having regard to the purpose for which the building is used, it would not be right for him to continue in occupation of the dwelling house.

Ground 8: Temporary housing during repairs

The dwelling-house was made available for occupation by the tenant (or a predecessor in title of his) while works were carried out on the dwelling-house which he previously occupied as his only or principal home and –

- the tenant (or predecessor) was a secure tenant of the other dwelling-house at the time when he ceased to occupy it as his home,
- the tenant (or predecessor) accepted the tenancy of the dwelling-house of which possession is sought on the understanding that he would give up occupation when, on completion of the works, the other dwelling-house was again available for occupation by him under a secure tenancy, and
- the works have been completed and the other dwelling-house is so available.

Grounds 9 - 11: Grounds on which the Court may order possession if suitable alternative accommodation is available
Ground 9: Overcrowding

The dwelling-house is overcrowded within the meaning of Part X, in such circumstances as to render the occupier guilty of an offence.

Ground 10: Demolition, reconstruction, or major works

The landlord intends , within a reasonable time of obtaining possession of the dwelling-house-

■ to demolish or reconstruct the building or part of the building comprising the dwelling-house, or

■ to carry out work on that building or on land let together with, and thus treated as part of, the dwelling-house,

■ and cannot reasonably do so without obtaining possession of the dwelling-house.

Ground 10A: Redevelopment scheme

The dwelling house is in an area which is the subject of a redevelopment scheme approved by the Secretary of State or the Housing Corporation in accordance with Part V of this Schedule and the landlord intends within a reasonable time of obtaining possession to dispose of the dwelling-house in accordance with this scheme.

or

Part of the dwelling-house is in such an area and the landlord intends within a reasonable time of obtaining possession to dispose of that part in accordance with the scheme and for that purpose reasonably requires possession of the dwelling-house.

Ground 11: Charitable landlord

The landlord is a charity and the tenant's continued occupation of the dwelling house would conflict with the objects of the charity.

Grounds 12 - 16: Grounds on which the Court may order possession if it considers it reasonable and suitable alternative accommodation is available

Ground 12: Tied accommodation

The dwelling-house forms part of, or is within the curtilage of, a building which, or so much of it as is held by the landlord, is held mainly for the purposes other than housing purposes and consists mainly of accommodation other than housing accommodation, or is situated in a cemetery, and-

- the dwelling-house was let to the tenant or a predecessor in title of his in consequence of the tenant or predecessor being in the employment of the landlord or of a local authority, a new town corporation a housing action trust, an urban development corporation the Development Board for Rural Wales, or the governors of an aided school, and that employment has ceased, and

- the landlord reasonably requires the dwelling-house for occupation as a residence for some person either engaged in the employment of the landlord, or of such a body, or with whom a contract for such employment has been entered into conditional on housing being provided.

Ground 13: Accommodation for disabled persons

The dwelling-house has features which are substantially different from those of ordinary dwelling-houses and which are designed to make it suitable for occupation by a physically disabled person who requires accommodation of a kind provided by the dwelling-house and- there is no longer such a person residing in the dwelling-house, and the landlord requires it for occupation (whether alone or with members of his family) by such a person.

Ground 14: Accommodation for special groups

The landlord is a housing association or housing trust which lets dwelling-houses only for occupation (whether alone or with others) by persons whose circumstances (other than merely financial circumstances) make it especially difficult for them to satisfy their need for housing, and-

- either there is no longer such a person residing in the dwelling-house or the tenant has received from a local housing authority an offer of accommodation in premises

38

which are to be let as a separate dwelling-house under a secure tenancy, and

- the landlord requires the dwelling-house for occupation (whether alone or with members of his family) by such a person.

Ground 15: Accommodation for special needs

The dwelling-house is one of a group of dwelling-houses which it is the practice of the landlord to let for occupation by persons with special needs-

- a social service or special facility is provided in close proximity to the group of dwelling-houses in order to assist in persons with those special needs,

- there is no longer a person with those special needs residing in the dwelling-house, and

- the landlord requires the dwelling-house for occupation (whether alone or with members of his family) by a person who has those special needs.

Ground 16: Under-occupation by successor

The accommodation afforded by the dwelling-house is more extensive than is reasonably required by the tenant and- the tenancy vested in the tenant by virtue of section 89 (succession to periodic tenancy), the tenant being qualified to succeed by virtue of section 87(b) (members of family other than spouse), and

- notice of the proceedings for possession was served under section 83 (or, where no such notice was served, the proceedings for possession were begun) more than six months but less than twelve months after the date of the previous tenant's death.

- The matter to be taken into account by the court in determining whether it is reasonable to make an order on this ground include-the age of the tenant, the period during which the tenant has occupied the dwelling-house as his only or principal home, and any financial or other support given by the tenant to the previous tenant.

****

4

ASSURED TENANCIES

The assured tenant

As we have seen, with the exception of local authority tenancies and a few remaining Rent Act protected tenancies, all tenancies, (with the main exceptions detailed), signed after Jan 15th 1989, are known as assured tenancies. An assured shorthold tenancy, which is the most common form of tenancy used by private landlords nowadays, is one type of assured tenancy, and is for a fixed term of six months minimum and can be brought to an end with two months notice by serving a section 21 (of the Housing Act 1988) notice.

It is important to note that all tenancies signed after February 1997 are assured shorthold agreements unless otherwise stated in the agreement.

Assured tenancies are governed by the 1988 Housing Act, as amended by the 1996 Housing Act. It is to these Acts, or outlines of the Acts that the tenant must refer when intending to sign a tenancy for a residential property.

For a tenancy to be assured, three conditions must be fulfilled:

- The premises must be a dwelling house. This basically means any premises which can be lived in. Business premises will normally fall outside this interpretation.

- There must exist a particular relationship between landlord and tenant. In other words there must exist a tenancy agreement. For example, a licence to occupy, as in the case of students, or accommodation occupied as a result of work, cannot be seen as a tenancy. Following on from this, the accommodation must be let as a single unit. The tenant, who must be an individual, must normally be able to sleep, cook and eat in the accommodation. Sharing of bathroom facilities will not prevent a tenancy being an assured tenancy but shared cooking or other facilities, such as a living room, will.

- The third requirement for an assured tenancy is that the tenant must occupy the dwelling as his or her only or principal home. In situations involving joint tenants at least one of them must occupy.

Tenancies that are not assured

A tenancy agreement will not be assured if one of the following conditions applies:

-The tenancy or the contract was entered into before 15th January 1989;

-If no rent is payable or if only a low rent amounting to less than two thirds of the present ratable value of the property is payable;

-If the premises are let for business purposes or for mixed residential and business purposes;

-If part of the dwelling house is licensed for the sale of liquor for consumption on the premises. This does not include the publican who lets out a flat;

-If the dwelling house is let with more than two acres of agricultural land;

-If the dwelling house is part of an agricultural holding and is occupied in relation to carrying out work on the holding;

-If the premises are let by a specified institution to students, i.e., halls of residence;

-If the premises are let for the purpose of a holiday;

-Where there is a resident landlord, e.g., in the case where the landlord has let one of his rooms but continues to live in the house;

-If the landlord is the Crown or a government department. Certain lettings by the Crown are capable of being assured, such as some lettings by the Crown Estate Commissioners;

-If the landlord is a local authority, a fully mutual housing association (this is where you have to be a shareholder to be a tenant) a newly created Housing Action Trust or any similar body listed in the 1988 Housing Act.

-If the letting is transitional such as a tenancy continuing in its original form until phased out, such as:

-A protected tenancy under the 1977 Rent Act;
-Secure tenancy granted before 1st January 1989, e.g., from a local authority or housing association. These tenancies are governed by the 1985 Housing Act.

The Assured Shorthold tenancy

The assured shorthold tenancy as we have seen, is the most common form of tenancy used in the private sector. The main principle of the assured shorthold tenancy is that it is issued for a period of six months minimum and can be brought to an end by the landlord serving two-months notice on the tenant. At the end of the six-month period the tenant, if given two months prior notice, must leave.

Any property let on an assured tenancy can be let on an assured shorthold, providing the following three conditions are met:

- The tenancy must be for a fixed term of not less than six months.
- The agreement cannot contain powers which enable the landlord to end the tenancy before six months. This does not include the right of the landlord to enforce the grounds for possession, which will be approximately the same as those for the assured tenancy (see below).
- A notice requiring possession at the end of the term is usually served two months before that date.
- A notice must be served before any rent increase giving one months clear notice and providing details of the rent increase.

If the landlord wishes to get possession of his/her property, in this case before the expiry of the contractual term, the landlord has to gain a court order. A notice of seeking possession must be served, giving fourteen days notice and following similar grounds of possession as an assured tenancy. *The landlord cannot simply tell a tenant to leave before the end of the agreed term.*

If the tenancy runs on after the end of the fixed term then the landlord can regain possession by giving the required two months notice, as mentioned above. At the end of the term for which the assured shorthold tenancy has been granted, the landlord has an automatic right to possession.

An assured shorthold tenancy will become periodic (will run from week to week) when the initial term of six months has elapsed and the landlord has not brought the tenancy to an end. A periodic tenancy is brought to an end with two months notice.

Assured shorthold tenants can be evicted only on certain grounds, some discretionary, some mandatory (see below).

In order for the landlord of an assured shorthold tenant to regain possession of the property, a notice of seeking possession (of property) must be served, giving fourteen days notice of expiry and stating the ground for possession.

Following the fourteen days a court order must be obtained. Although gaining a court order is not complicated, a solicitor will usually be used. Court costs can be awarded against the tenant.

Security of tenure: The ways in which a tenant can lose their home as an assured tenant

There are a number of circumstances called grounds (mandatory and discretionary) whereby a landlord can start a court action to evict a tenant.

The following are the *mandatory* grounds (where the judge must give the landlord possession) and *discretionary* grounds (where the judge does not have to give the landlord possession) on which a court can order possession if the home is subject to an assured tenancy.

The mandatory grounds for possession of a property let on an assured tenancy

There are eight mandatory grounds for possession, which, if proved, leave the court with no choice but to make an order for possession. It is very important that you understand these.

Ground One is used where the landlord has served a notice, no later than at the beginning of the tenancy, warning the tenant that this ground may be used against him/her. This ground is used where the landlord wishes to recover the property as his or her principal (first and only) home or the spouse's (wife's or husbands) principal home.

The ground is not available to a person who bought the premises for gain (profit) whilst they were occupied.

Ground Two is available where the property is subject to a mortgage and if the landlord does not pay the mortgage, could lose the home.

Grounds Three and Four relate to holiday lettings.

Ground Five is a special one, applicable to ministers of religion.

Ground Six relates to the demolition or reconstruction of the property.

Ground Seven applies if a tenant dies and in his will leaves the tenancy to someone else: but the landlord must start proceedings against the new tenant within a year of the death if he wants to evict the new tenant.

Ground Eight concerns rent arrears. This ground applies if, both at the date of the serving of the notice seeking possession and at the date of the hearing of the action, the rent is at least 8 weeks in arrears or two months in arrears. This is the main ground used by landlords when rent is not being paid.

The discretionary grounds for possession of a property, which is let on an assured tenancy

As we have seen, the discretionary grounds for possession are those in relation to which the court has some powers over whether or not the landlord can evict. In other words, the final decision is left to the judge. Often the judge will prefer to grant a suspended order first, unless the circumstances are dramatic.

Ground Nine applies when suitable alternative accommodation is available or will be when the possession order takes effect. As we have seen, if the landlord wishes to obtain possession of his or her property in order to use it for other purposes then suitable alternative accommodation has to be provided.

Ground Ten deals with rent arrears as does *ground eleven.* These grounds are distinct from the mandatory grounds, as there does not have to be a fixed arrear in terms of time scale, e.g., 8 weeks.

The judge, therefore, has some choice as to whether or not to evict. In practice, this ground will not be relevant to managers of assured shorthold tenancies.

Ground Twelve concerns any broken obligation of the tenancy. As we have seen with the protected tenancy, there are a number of conditions of the tenancy agreement, such as the requirement not to racially or sexually harass a neighbor. Ground Twelve will be used if these conditions are broken.

Ground Thirteen deals with the deterioration of the dwelling as a result of a tenant's neglect. This is connected with the structure of the property and is the same as for a protected tenancy. It puts the responsibility on the tenant to look after the premises.

Ground Fourteen concerns nuisance, annoyance and illegal or immoral use. This is where a tenant or anyone connected with the tenant has caused a nuisance to neighbors.

Ground 14A this ground deals with domestic violence.

Ground 15 concerns the condition of the furniture and tenants neglect. As Ground thirteen puts some responsibility on the tenant to look after the structure of the building so Ground Fifteen makes the tenant responsible for the furniture and fittings.

Ground 16 covers former employees. The premises were let to a former tenant by a landlord seeking possession and the tenant has ceased to be in that employment.

Ground 17 is where a person or that persons agents makes a false Or reckless statement and this has caused the landlord to grant the tenancy under false pretences.

The description of the grounds above is intended as a guide only. For a fuller description please refer to the 1988 Housing Act, section 7, Schedule two,) as amended by the 1996 Housing Act) which is available at reference libraries.

Fast track possession

In November 1993, following changes to the County Court Rules, a facility was introduced which enabled landlords of tenants with assured shorthold tenancies to apply for possession of their property without the usual time delay involved in waiting for a court date and attendance at court. This is known as "fast track possession" It cannot be used for rent arrears or other grounds. It is used to gain possession of a property when the fixed term of six months or more has come to an end and the tenant will not move.

Payment of rent

If the landlord wishes to raise rent, at least one month's minimum notice must be given. The rent cannot be raised more than once for the same tenant in one year. Tenants have the right to challenge a rent increase if they think it is unfair by referring the rent to a Rent Assessment Committee. The committee will prevent the landlord from raising the rent above the ordinary market rent for that type of property. We will be discussing rent and rent control further on in this book.

5

JOINT TENANCIES

Joint tenancies: the position of two or more people who have a tenancy agreement for one property

Although it is the normal state of affairs for a tenancy agreement to be granted to one person, this is not always the case.

A tenancy can also be granted to two or more people and is then known as a *joint tenancy*. The position of joint tenants is exactly the same as that of single tenants. In other words, there is still one tenancy even though it is shared.

Each tenant is responsible for paying the rent and observing the terms and conditions of the tenancy agreement. No one joint tenant can prevent another joint tenants access to the premises.

If one of the joint tenants dies then his or her interest will automatically pass to the remaining joint tenants. A joint tenant cannot dispose of his or her interest in a will.

If one joint tenant, however, serves a notice to quit (notice to leave the property) on another joint tenant(s) then the tenancy will come to an end and the landlord can apply to court for a possession order, if the remaining tenant does not leave.

The position of a wife or husband in relation to joint tenancies is rather more complex because the married person has more rights when it comes to the home than the single person.

Remember: the position of a tenant who has signed a joint tenancy agreement is exactly the same as that of the single tenant. If one person leaves, the other(s) have the responsibilities of the tenancy. If one person leaves without paying his share of the rent then the other tenants will have to pay instead.

6

MOBILE HOMES

If you own a mobile home, rent a pitch for it on a site and use it as your main residence, you will be protected by the Mobile Homes Act 1983. If you rent the home you will be covered by the law for tenants. The Act does not cover you if you only rent the home for holidays.

Protection from eviction
The Mobile Homes Act 1983 gives owners the right to keep their homes on the site they occupy indefinitely. There can only be a fixed time limit on the agreement if the site owner's planning permission, or right to use the land, is itself limited to a fixed period. If the time limit is later extended, then so is your right to stay there. The resident can bring the agreement to an end by giving at least four weeks notice in writing. The site owner can only bring the agreement to an end by applying to the county court or to an arbitrator. There are only three grounds on which the site owner can seek to end an agreement:

- You are not living in the mobile home as your main residence.
- The mobile home is having a detrimental effect on the site because of its age or condition or is likely to have this effect within the next five years. The site owner can only try to use this ground for ending the agreement once in any five-year period, starting from the date the agreement began.
- You have broken one of the terms of the agreement and the court or the arbitrator thinks it is reasonable to end the agreement. The site owner must first tell you that you have

broken the agreement and give you a reasonable time to put things right.

If the site owner can prove to the court or the arbitrator that the agreement should be brought to an end for one of these reasons, the site owner can then get an eviction order from the courts. Arbitrators cannot make eviction orders. The site owner can normally go to court to end the agreement and for an eviction order at the same time.

If the site is privately owned, the court can suspend an eviction order for up to one year, but cannot suspend it if the site is owned by the local council. It is a criminal offence for the site owner to evict you without a court order, to harass or threaten you or to cut off services such as gas, electricity or water in order to get you to leave.

The site owner can only make you move to another part of the site if:

- Your agreement says that this can be done
- The new pitch is broadly comparable to the old one
- The site owner pays all the costs.

The right to a written agreement and a statement of rights

The site owner must give you a statement of your legal rights and the terms of your agreement. The agreement cannot change your rights under the Mobile Homes Act. You or the site owner can apply to change the terms of the agreement within six months of the issue of the original agreement. Either side can apply to the county court or an arbitrator, if they cannot agree the terms. You should always check the agreement for the terms of payment and fees and if not happy apply to change them.

Other rights of mobile home owners

You can sell your home and pass on the agreement with the site owner to a person of your choice. You can also give your home to a member of your family. In either case, the new owner must be approved by the site owner, but this approval cannot be unreasonably withheld. If this is the case then you can apply to the county court or an arbitrator for an order for the site owner to give approval. If you sell your home the site owner can claim a commission of up to 20% of the price. If you die members of your family who were living with you will automatically inherit the agreement with the site owner and your legal rights.

7

AGRICULTURAL TENANCIES

The Agricultural Tenancies Act 1995 changed the nature of agricultural tenancies. From 1st September 1995, no more tenancies of 'agricultural holdings have been granted and agricultural tenancies came to be known as 'Farm Business tenancies' having much more in common with the 1954 LTA than it does with previous agricultural Acts such as the Agricultural Holdings Act of 1986. At its heart, the 1995 Act has the notion of freedom of contract. Parties are free to negotiate the tenancy on whatever terms suit them. The act imposes no more security of tenure beyond the length of the tenancy agreed between landlord and tenant. There are no rights of succession.

Definition of Farm Business Tenancy

A tenancy will be a farm business tenancy for the purposes of the 1995 Act if it meets the business conditions together with either the agricultural condition or the notice conditions (s1 (1) (a). It cannot be a farm business tenancy if it began before September 1st 1995 or if the tenancy is an agricultural holding, There are certain tenancies which may be agricultural holdings if they began after September 1st if they fall within the exceptions set out in s4. These include:

(a) where the tenancy begins after 1st September but pursuant to a written contract of tenancy entered into before that date which indicates that the 1986 Act is to apply in relation to that tenancy (s4 (1) (a);

(b) where the tenancy was obtained under the right of succession contained within the 1986 Act;: whether the tenancy was obtained by a direction of the ALT under s 39 or s53 of the 1986 Act, granted by the landlord under s 45 (6) of the 1986 Act following a direction of the ALT or granted by a written contract of tenancy following an agreement with the landlord:

(c) where the tenancy was granted under the 'Evesham custom':

(d) where the tenancy was granted to someone who immediately before the grant was the tenant of the holding (or a substantial part of the holding under the 1986 Act and the new tenancy was not expressly granted but had effect as an implied surrender and re-grant of the tenancy though the purpose was only to vary the lease.

Business conditions

There are two business conditions:

(a) that all or part of the land comprised in the tenancy is farmed for the purposes of a trade or business, and

(b) that since the beginning of the tenancy all or part of the land has been so farmed.

Both conditions must be satisfied. The business conditions do not require that the same part of the land is always farmed for the purposes of a trade or business: they will be satisfied even if different parts of the land have been used for commercial farming at different times, provided that at all times some part of the land has been farmed for the purposes of a trade or business.

If during the course of a tenancy the land ceases to be used for agricultural activity, the business condition will cease to be satisfied and the tenancy will fall outside of the 1995 Act. However, if the land continues to be used for a commercial purposes then it may still qualify as a business tenancy under the 1954 LTA.

The agriculture condition

S 1 (3) of the 1995 Act states that the agricultural condition is that, having regard to:

(a) the terms of the tenancy

(b) the use of the land comprised in the tenancy

(c) the nature of any commercial activities carried on that land

(d) any other relevant circumstances

The character of the tenancy is primarily or wholly agricultural.

Unlike the business conditions, the agricultural conditions do not have to have been satisfied since the beginning of the tenancy, it only needs to have been satisfied since the beginning of the proceedings. However, it does require that the tenancy is primarily or wholly agricultural.

The notice conditions

The notice conditions make sure that the tenancy will remain a farm business tenancy. To satisfy the notice conditions there are two requirements. The first is that, on or before the relevant day, the landlord and tenant each gave each other a written notice:

(a) identifying the land to be comprised in the tenancy and:

(b) containing a statement to the effect that the person giving the notice intends the tenancy or proposed tenancy is to be, and remain, a farm business tenancy (s 1)4) (a)

The relevant day is defined in s 1(5) as whichever is the earlier of the following:

(a) the day on which the parties enter into any instrument creating the tenancy, other than an agreement to enter into a tenancy on a future date, or

(b) the beginning of the tenancy.

The second requirement is that, at the beginning of the tenancy the character of the tenancy was primarily or wholly agricultural (s 1 (4) (b). This requirement of the notice condition needs only to be satisfied at the beginning of the tenancy. Provided that notice has properly been served it does not matter if the tenancy moves away from agriculture. The tenancy will remain a farm business tenancy provided that a part of the land is used for agriculture.

Terminating a farm business tenancy

The ATA 1995 affords minimal security of tenure for farm business tenancies. The basic protection is given through the time periods imposed when serving notice to quit. These are contained within sections 5 6 and 7 of the Act. No grounds for possession are needed, unlike assured or secure tenancies.

Fixed term tenancies of two years or more:

Section 5 (1) provides that:

..A farm business tenancy for a term of two years or more shall, instead of terminating on the term date, continue (as from that date) as a tenancy from year to year but otherwise on the terms of the original tenancy so far as applicable, unless at least twelve months but not less than twenty four months before the term date a written notice has been given by either party to the other of his intention to terminate the tenancy.

As in the Agricultural Holding Act 1986, the 1995 Act ensures the continuation of longer-term fixed term tenancies. Such tenancies require a year's notice of termination. It is not possible to contract out of the provisions of s 5. The provisions apply to both landlord and tenant.

Fixed term tenancies of two years or less

These tenancies have no protection under the 1995 act and will expire at the end of the term.

Tenancies from year to year

Section 6 (1) of the 1995 Act provides:

Where a farm business tenancy is a tenancy from year to year, a notice to quit the holding or part of the holding shall be invalid unless:

(a) it is in writing
(b) it is to take effect at the end of a year of tenancy, and
(c) it is given at least twelve months but less than twenty-four months before the date on which it is to take effect.

Thus a tenancy from year to year will be subject to twelve months notice as a minimum.

Sub-tenants

The 1995 Act gives no protection to sub-tenants. If the head tenancy is terminated by notice to quit then sub-tenancies will also be terminated.

Joint tenants

If a landlord serves a notice to quit on any one of a number of sub-tenants, or one joint tenant serves notice to quit on the landlord, this will determine the joint tenancy.

Licensees

The 1995 Act offers no protection for licensees and they will fall outside its provisions. However, the rule laid out in street v Mountford will apply and any agreement purporting to be a licence which grants exclusive occupation at a rent will in fact be a tenancy.

Rent

The position with regard to rent in a farm business tenancy is determined by the law of contract, or the underlying principles of freedom of contract. The parties are free to agree between them what the level of rent should be and also periods for variation of rent. The Act does supply a mechanism for arbitration but also allows parties to opt out of these provisions. The statutory rent review provisions will not come into force where the tenancy agreement states that the remit will not be reviewed during the period, where the agreement states that tie rent will be varied at a specified time by a specified amount and also where ether agreement states that the rent shall be varied at specified times using a formula.

Statutory rent increase provisions

Under the 1995 Act, either the landlord or tenant can demand a rent review every three years. This is done by serving a statutory review notice on the other party requiring the rent to be referred to arbitration. The review date must be at least twelve months but less than 24 months after the day on which the statutory review notice is given. Where there is no agreement in writing, the review date will be the anniversary of the beginning of the tenancy unless the landlord and tenant agree in writing that it is to be some other date and the three year period will run from the latest of the following dates:

(a) the beginning of the new tenancy
(b) the date as from which there took effect a previous direction of an arbitrator as to the amount of rent
(c) the date as from which there took affect a previous agreement in writing between the landlord and tenant, entered into since the grant of tenancy, as to the amount of rent.

Even if there is an agreement in writing re the rent the matter can still be referred to tribunal.

Severance of the landlord's reversion

Section 11 makes special provisions with regard to the severance of the landlord's reversion. If the landlord sells part of his estate which is let to a tenant under a farm business tenancy and as a result of severing the estate a new tenancy of part of the land is granted to the tenant, the three year period between statutory rent reviews will run from the granting of tie original tenancy not from the creation of the new tenancy.

Compensation for improvements

Section 16 gives a farm business tenant the right, subject to certain conditions being fulfilled, to be entitled on the termination of the tenancy, to obtain from the landlord compensation for any tenants improvements s 16 (1). Tenant's improvements mean any physical improvement which is made on the holding by the tenant wholly or partly at his or her expense. It also means any intangible advantage which is obtained for the holding by the tenant by his own effort or wholly or partly at his own expense. The right does not arise in respect of any physical improvement which is removed from the holding or any intangible advantage which does not remain attached to the holding.

Compensation will only be available if the tenant has obtained landlords consent for improvements. The consent should be in writing s (17)1. If a landlord fails to give consent for an improvement, or fails within two months of the request in writing or requires the tenant to agree to a variation in terms as a condition of giving consent then the tenant may notify the landlord in writing that he or she wishes to apply for arbitration under s 19. s19 will only apply if the tenant gives notice in writing before commencing the improvement, except where the improvement is a routine improvement. This is defined as an improvement made in the normal course of farming the holding or any part of the building which does not consist of fixed equipment or an improvement to fixed equipment (s19(10).

Landlords consent for planning permission

Where planning permission is required for the tenants improvement special conditions apply regarding landlords consent. The tenant will only be entitled to compensation if:

(a) the landlord has given his consent in writing to the making of the application for planning permission and;

(b) that consent is expressed to be given for the purpose of enabling the tenant to make a specified physical improvement to the holding or of enabling the tenant lawfully to effect a specified change of use and;

(c) on the termination of the tenancy, the specified physical improvement has not been completed or the specified change of use has not been effected (s 18(11).

The amount of compensation for improvements will be an amount equal to the increase attributable to the improvement in the value of the holding at the termination of the tenancy. This amount will be reduced where the landlord has agreed to contribute part of the costs of improvements.

Protection of Residential Agricultural workers

So far, we have dealt with the commercial letting of agricultural land. However, a different area of law is the residential protection of agricultural workers. This is specifically where a premises is supplied as part of the job.

In order for an occupier to acquire an assured agricultural occupancy or protection under the Rent (Agriculture) Act 1976 it is an essential requirement that the premises is either arranged or owned by the occupier's employer.

This, however, will not always be the case. Many agricultural workers will be tenants like any other tenants and may acquire protection under the Housing Act 1988 or the Rent Act 1977 depending on when the tenancy was granted. The fact that they work in the field of agriculture will not make any difference.

The main Acts to be considered are the 1976 Rent (Agriculture) Act and Chapter 111 of the 1988 Housing Act.

The Rent (Agriculture) Act 1976

Tenancies and licences granted before 15th January 1989 will be governed by the Rent (Agriculture) Act 1976. In order to fall within the protection of this Act a number of definitions must be satisfied. The agricultural worker must be a 'qualifying worker', the tenancy or licence must be a 'relevant' tenancy or licence and the dwelling house in question must be in 'qualifying ownership'.

Qualifying worker

A person is a qualifying worker for the purposes of the act at any time, if at that time he or she has worked for the whole time in agriculture for not less than ninety-one percent of the last 104 weeks (Sch 3 para 1). A person can also be within the protection of the Act if he or she is incapable of work because of a disease or accident arising as a result of their work.

Agriculture

'Agriculture' is defined by s 1 (1) of the 1976 Act to include dairy farming, livestock keeping and breeding, the production of any consumable produce and the use of land for grazing, pasture, orchards, market gardens, nurseries and forestry. This is not an exhaustive list. For example, a person employed to repair farm machinery is employed in agriculture (McPhail v Greensmith (1993) 2 EGLR 228 CA but a gamekeeper is not (Normanton (Earl of) v Giles (1980) 1 WLR 28 HL.

Relevant licence and relevant tenancy

A relevant tenancy is a tenancy of a separate dwelling which would be a protected tenancy under the Rent Act 1977 but for the provisions of the 1977 Act listed below. A relevant tenancy may not be a tenancy which falls under Part 11 of the Landlord and Tenant Act 1954 (business tenancies), part 1 of the 1954 Act or Sch 10 to the Local Government and Housing Act 1989 (long leases).

A relevant licence is any licence under which a person has the exclusive occupation of a dwelling house as a separate dwelling which, if it were a tenancy, would be a protected tenancy under the Rent Act 1977 but for the provisions of the 1977 Act listed below.

The provisions of the 1977 Rent Act are:
(a) s 5 (which excludes tenancies at low rents, see 13.44) (Sch 2 para 3(2)
(b) s 10 (which excludes a tenancy of a dwelling house which is comprised in an agricultural tenancy holding which is occupied by the person responsible for the control of the farming of the holding, see 13.65 (Sch 2, para 3(2).
(c) S 7 (which excludes a tenancy where the rent includes payment for board or attendance, see 13.51) The 1976 Act modifies this section to make it clear that meals provided in the course of a persons employment in agriculture do not constitute 'board' (Sch 2, para 3).

Protected occupier
Section 2(1) and (2) of the 1976 Act provide that a person will be a protected occupier in his or her own right (as opposed to by succession) where:

(a) he or she holds a relevant licence or a relevant tenancy in relation to a dwelling house, and
(b) the dwelling house is in qualifying ownership or has been in qualifying ownership at any time during the subsistence of the licence or tenancy (whether it was at the time a relevant licence or tenancy or not) and either:

(i)   he or she is a qualifying worker, or
(ii)   he or she has been a qualifying worker at any time during the subsistence of the licence or the tenancy (whether at the time it was a relevant licence or tenancy or not), or
(iii)   he or she is incapable of whole time work in agriculture in consequence of a qualifying injury or disease.

Security of tenure
The system of security of tenure offered under the 1976 Act is very similar to that offered by the Rent Act 1977. S 4 (1) of the 1976 Act provides that when a protected occupiers tenancy or licence is

terminated, and the tenant or licensee continues to occupy the dwelling house as his residence, a statutory tenancy will arise. The protected occupiers licence or tenancy may be terminated by a notice to quit, a notice of increase of rent under s 16(3) of the act or otherwise.

A court may not make an order for possession of a dwelling house subject to a protected tenancy or a statutory tenancy unless the landlord can establish one of the statutory grounds for possession set out in Sch 4 (s6 (1). As under the Rent Act 1977 these are divided into discretionary and mandatory grounds. In the case of discretionary grounds the court will not make an order for possession unless it considers it reasonable to do so. The court also has power to adjourn. It can also stay or suspend the execution of an order or postpone date of possession.

Discretionary Grounds under the 1976 Act:

1. That suitable alternative accommodation is, or will be available
2. That the housing authority has offered to provide or arrange suitable alternative accommodation
3. That the tenant has not paid rent lawfully due
4. That the tenant is guilty of annoyance or nuisance to neighbours
5. That the condition of the dwelling house has deteriorated due to the tenants actions
6. That the condition of furniture has deteriorated due to actions of the tenant
7. That the tenant has given notice to quit and the tenant would be seriously prejudiced if he could not obtain possession.
8. That the tenant has sub let or assigned without permission
9. That the dwelling house is reasonably required for occupation by the landlord
10. That the tenant is overcharging a sub-tenant.

Mandatory grounds

The landlord must show:

(a) that before granting the tenancy the person who granted the tenancy (the original occupier) occupied the dwelling house as his or her only or principal home and the court is now satisfied that the dwelling house is now required as a residence for the original occupier or member of family who lived with the original occupier when he or she last occupied the property and the original occupier gave notice to the tenant before the start of the tenancy that possession might be recovered under this case.

(b) That the person who granted the tenancy acquired the dwelling house with a view to occupying it as a residence on his or her retirement, that person has now retired and requires the dwelling house as his or her residence or that they have died and it is required for a member of the family and that notice was given to the tenant before the start of the tenancy that possession might be recovered under this case.

(c) That the dwelling house is overcrowded within the meaning of part X of the Housing Act 1985 in such circumstances as to render the occupier guilty of an offence.

Rent

With a protected tenancy in employment a low rent or no rent at all will usually be applicable. This will not the case when a protected tenancy is terminated and a statutory tenancy begins. Rent will only be payable when a statutory tenancy arises if the landlord and tenant fix the rent by agreement under s 11 of the Act or the landlord serves a notice of increase of rent under s 12 or s 14 of the act.

As under the Rent Act 1977, both parties have the right to apply to register a fair rent.

Succession

The 1976 Act provides for a single succession. Where the deceased was a protected occupier in his or her own right (i.e. not by succession) his or her spouse, providing he or she was resident with the tenant immediately before death, and has a relevant licence or tenancy, will succeed to the protected tenancy. If there is no spouse, a member of the deceased's family can succeed providing that they resided with the deceased six months before the death. Where the protected tenancy has been terminated and the deceased is a statutory tenant the situation is different. A spouse may succeed to a statutory tenancy as may a family member who has resided with the deceased for two years before death. However, a family member, in contrast to a spouse, will succeed to an assured tenancy under the Housing Act 1988.

Assured Agricultural occupancies

Tenancies and licences granted to agricultural workers after 125th January 1989 will be governed by Chapter 111 of the Housing Act 1988.

In order to be an assured agricultural occupancy the tenancy or licence of the dwelling house must be:

(a) an assured tenancy which is not an assured shorthold tenancy

(b) a tenancy which would be an assured tenancy but for the fact that it is excluded by:

    (i) the provision of Sch1, para 3, 3A and 3B which exclude tenancies at low rent or

    (ii) the provision of Sch1, para 7 which excludes a tenancy of a dwelling house which is comprised in an agricultural holding or farm business tenancy which is occupied by the person responsible for the control of the farming or management of the holding, or

(c) a licence under which a person has exclusive occupation of a dwelling house as a separate dwelling which, if it were a tenancy, would satisfy (a) or (b) above.

Agricultural worker condition

The first requirement of the agricultural worker condition is that the dwelling house must be in a qualifying ownership or have been in qualifying ownership at any time during the subsistence of the tenancy or licence (whether or not it was at that time a relevant tenancy or licence). Qualifying ownership is defined as under the 1976 Act.

The second requirement is that the occupier (or where there are joint occupiers at least one of them):

(a) is a qualifying worker or has been a qualifying worker at any time during the subsistence of the tenancy or licence (whether or not it was at that time a relevant tenancy or licence): or

(b) is incapable of whole time work (or work as a permit worker) in agriculture in consequence of a qualifying disease.

Where the agricultural worker condition is fulfilled and the tenant or licensee is granted another relevant tenancy or licence of another dwelling house in consideration of giving up possession of the original dwelling house, the tenant or licensee will continue to satisfy the agricultural worker condition.

Succession

The agricultural worker condition may also be fulfilled by succession. This will occur where a dwelling house is subject to a relevant tenancy or licence and an occupier who satisfied the agricultural worker condition has died. A spouse may succeed where she was residing with the deceased at the time of his or her death and, if there is no spouse, a member of the family may succeed if they were residing g with the deceased for the period of two years before his or her death.

Security of tenure

Where the tenancy or licence is a relevant tenancy or licence and the agricultural worker condition is fulfilled, the tenancy or licence will be an assured agricultural occupancy. An assured agricultural occupancy which is not an assured tenancy will be treated as if it were an assured tenancy (s24 (3) with the following alterations:

(a) a landlord will not be entitled to seek possession of the dwelling house under ground 16

(b) if the tenant gives notice to terminate his or her employment, that notice shall not constitute a notice to quit notwithstanding any agreement to the contrary

(c) when an assured agricultural tenancy is terminated and a statutory periodic tenancy arises by virtue of s 5 that statutory periodic tenancy will be an assured agricultural occupancy as long as the agricultural condition is for the time being fulfilled with respect to the dwelling house in question

(d) if no rent is payable under an assured agricultural occupancy the statutory tenancy that arises on termination of then occupancy will be a monthly periodic tenancy.

Assured shorthold tenancies

Since the introduction of assured shorthold tenancies in the 1988 Housing Act many agricultural workers have been granted shortholds which provides a simple way of gaining recovery of a property.

8

RENT AND CHARGES

The payment of rent and other financial matters

If a tenancy is protected under the Rent Act 1977, as described earlier there is the right to apply to the Rent Officer for the setting of a fair rent for the property.

The assured tenant

The assured tenant has far fewer rights in relation to rent control than the protected tenant.

The Housing Act 1988 allows a landlord to charge whatever he likes. There is no right to a fair or reasonable rent with an assured tenancy. If the tenancy is assured then there will usually be a formula in the tenancy which will provide guidance for rent increases. If not then the landlord can set what rent he or she likes within reason. If the amount is unreasonable then the tenant can refer the matter to the rent assessment committee. The rent can sometimes be negotiated at the outset of the tenancy. This rent has to be paid as long as the contractual term of the tenancy lasts. Once the contractual term has expired, the landlord is entitled to continue to charge the same rent.

On expiry of an assured shorthold the landlord is free to grant a new tenancy and set the rent to a level that is compatible with the market.

Rent control for assured shorthold tenants

We have seen that the assured shorthold tenancy is for a period of six months minimum. Like the assured tenant, the assured shorthold tenant has no right to request that a fair rent should be set. The rent is a market rent.

As with an assured tenancy, the assured shorthold tenant has the right to appeal to a Rent Assessment Committee in the case of what he/she considers an unreasonable rent. This may be done during the contractual term of the tenancy. The Committee will consider whether the rent is significantly higher than is usual for a similar property.

If the Committee assesses a different rent from that set by the landlord, they may set a date when the increase will take effect. The rent cannot be backdated to before the date of the application. Once a decision has been reached by the Committee, the landlord cannot increase the rent for at least twelve months, or on termination of the tenancy. Details of the local Rent Assessment Committee can be obtained from the Rent Officer Service at your local authority.

Housing benefit

Housing benefit is a means tested benefit available only to tenants who cannot pay their rent. It is available whether or not the tenant is in employment. Housing benefit is administered by the local authority who are in turn reimbursed by central government.

Local authorities will assess the level of rent in their areas. They use what are known as reference rents and will not pay above this level. This was introduced to curb excessive rents. In addition, rent will normally be paid to landlords direct in order to ensure that rent is paid and not spent on other things.

The rules for entitlement to housing benefit differ according to whether the tenant is in receipt of income support. In the case of income support, entitlement to housing benefit is automatic and the maximum benefit will be payable. For other claimants, entitlement is means tested and the general principle is that over a certain personal earnings limit corresponding reductions will apply. It is not only the claimants income that is relevant: capital over a certain limit will be deemed to be income. Also, other people living in the home will affect entitlement.

The basic rule for housing benefit is that the property must be the only or principal home, although temporary absence can be ignored. Entitlement to benefit is based on the amount of 'eligible' rent. This means that certain personal items, such as heating, lighting and water charges will not be eligible for rent.

Restrictions on the amount of benefit

As mentioned, the benefit payable may not be the full amount of eligible rent. This is to discourage claims for excessively large properties and high rents. The principle is that benefit is paid according to need. The rules governing the amount paid differ depending upon whether the applicant first became entitled to benefit before 2nd January 1996 or afterwards.

Previously, private sector rents were referred to the rent officer to determine whether or not they were a reasonable market rent. This no longer happens. In determining the reasonable market rent the rent officer will also take into account the size factor, the criteria of which are laid down. If the accommodation is significantly larger than the tenant and family, if relevant, need then the rent officer can set a lower figure, based on need. Local authorities will not always automatically limit the rent paid as they will, as appropriate take into account the needs of the family, for example disability.

The size criteria for calculating benefit are:

a) One bedroom for each of the following category of occupiers:
    - A married or unmarried couple
    - A person who is not a child
    - Two children of the same sex
    - Two children who are more than 10 years old
    - A child (person under 16)
b) The number of rooms (excluding any allowed as a bedroom) suitable for living in:

    - For fewer than four occupants, one
    - For more than three but fewer than seven occupants, two
    - In any other case, three.

Local authorities are asked to set a 'local reference rent' for the area. This is the average rent which the rent officer would expect a landlord to be able to obtain on a letting of a property in that locality to a tenant not claiming benefit. Rents are set on a needs basis.

There are other formula applied to the payment of housing benefit and the local authority will inform you of the criteria used on application for benefit.

Council tax and the tenant

From April 1993 the council tax replaced the poll tax. Unlike poll tax, the council tax is based on properties, or dwellings, and not individual people. This means that there is one bill for each individual dwelling, rather than separate bills for each person. The number and type of people who live in the dwelling may affect the size of the final bill. A discount of 25% is given for people who live alone. Each property is placed in a valuation band with different properties paying more or less depending on their individual value. Tenants who feel that their home has been placed in the wrong valuation band can appeal to their local authority council tax department.

Who has to pay the council tax?

In most cases the tenant occupying the dwelling will have to pay the council tax. However, a landlord will be responsible for paying the council tax where there are several households living in one dwelling. This will usually be hostels, bedsits and other non-self contained flats where people share things such as cooking and washing facilities. The council tax on this type of property remains the responsibility of the landlord even if all but one of the tenants move out. Although the landlord has the responsibility for paying the council tax, he/she will normally try to pass on the increased cost through rents. However, as we have seen, there is a set procedure for a landlord to follow if he/she wishes to increase rent.

Dwellings, which are exempt

Certain properties will be exempt from the council tax, such as student's halls of residences and nurse's homes. Properties with all students resident will be exempt from the tax. However, if one non-student moves in then that property will no longer be exempt from tax. Uninhabitable empty properties are exempt from tax, as they are not counted as dwellings.

This is not the same as homes, which have been declared as unfit for human habitation by Environmental Health officers. The deciding factor will be whether or not a property is capable of being lived in.

Reductions in council tax bills
Tenants in self-contained accommodation who live alone will be entitled to a discount of 25% of the total bill.

Tenants may also qualify for the discount if they share their homes with people who do not count for council tax purposes. Such people are: children under eighteen; students; patients resident in hospital; people who are severely mentally impaired; low paid careworkers; eighteen or nineteen year olds still at school (or just left); people in prison (except for non-payment of fines or the council tax); and people caring for someone with a disability who is not a spouse, partner or child under eighteen.

Council tax benefits available for those on low income
Tenants on very low income, except for students, will usually be able to claim council tax benefit. This can cover up to 100% of the council tax.

Tenants with disabilities may be entitled to further discounts. Tenants who are not responsible for individual council tax, but pay it through their rent, can claim housing benefit to cover the increase.

The rules covering council tax liability can be obtained from a Citizens Advice Bureau or from your local authority council tax department.

Service charges
A service charge covers provision of services other than those covered by the rent. A rental payment will normally cover

maintenance charges, loan charges if any, and also profit. Other services, such as cleaning and gardening, will be covered by a separate charge, known as a service charge. A *registered* rent reflects the cost of any services provided by the landlord. An assured rent set by a landlord will normally include services, which must be outlined in the agreement.

The fact that the charges are variable must be written into a tenancy agreement and the landlord has a legal duty to provide the tenant with annual budgets and accounts and has to consult when he or she wishes to spend over a certain amount of money, currently £250 per dwelling or £100 for contracts such as cleaning and lift maintenance if they are for more than 12 months.

The form of consultation, which must take place, is that of writing to all those affected and informing them of:

-The landlord's intention to carry out work;

-Why these works are seen to be necessary;

This first notice is for 30 days after which another notice must be sent containing:

-The estimated cost of the works;
-At least two estimates or the inviting of them to see two estimates.

A period of twenty-eight days must be allowed before work is carried out. This gives time for any feedback from tenants.

The landlord can incur reasonable expense, without consultation, if the work is deemed to be necessary, i.e. emergency works.

If a service charge is variable then a landlord has certain legal obligations, which are clearly laid out in the 1985 and 1987 Landlord and Tenant Acts as amended by the 2002 Commonhold and Leasehold Reform Act.

Deposits
A landlord can charge a *deposit*, to set against the possibility that a

tenant may damage the property or furniture. For most types of tenancy the law puts a limit on the amount that can be charged. The normal amount is 1 month's rent. The deposit must be lodged with one of a number of deposit protection schemes, after April 1st 2007. It is illegal not to do so.

9

THE RIGHT TO QUIET ENJOYMENT

Earlier, we saw that when a tenancy agreement is signed, the landlord is contracting to give quiet enjoyment of the tenants home. This means that they have the Right to live peacefully in the home without harassment.

The landlord is obliged not to do anything that will disturb the right to the quiet enjoyment of the home. The most serious breach of this right would be for the landlord to wrongfully evict a tenant.

Eviction: what can be done against unlawful harassment and eviction

It is a criminal offence for a landlord unlawfully to evict a residential occupier (whether or not a tenant!). The occupier has protection under the Protection from Eviction Act 1977 section 1(2).

If the tenant or occupier is unlawfully evicted his/her first course should be to seek an injunction compelling the landlord to readmit him/her to the premises. It is an unfortunate fact but many landlords will attempt to evict tenants forcefully. In doing so they break the law.

However, the landlord may, on termination of the tenancy recover possession without a court order if the agreement was entered into after 15th January 1989 and it falls into one of the following six situations:

- The occupier shares any accommodation with the landlord and the landlord occupies the premises as his or her only or principal home.
- The occupier shares any of the accommodation with a member of the landlords family, that person occupies the premises as their only or principal home, and the landlord occupies as his or her only or principal home premises in the same building.

- The tenancy or licence was granted temporarily to an occupier who entered the premises as a trespasser.
- The tenancy or licence gives the right to occupy for the purposes of a holiday.
- The tenancy or licence is rent-free.
- The licence relates to occupation of a hostel.

There is also a section in the 1977 Protection from Eviction Act which provides a defense for otherwise unlawful eviction and that is that the landlord may repossess if it is thought that the tenant no longer lives on the premises. It is important to note that, in order for such action to be seen as a crime under the 1977 Protection from Eviction Act, the intention of the landlord to evict must be proved.

However, there is another offence, namely harassment, which also needs to be proved. Even if the landlord is not guilty of permanently depriving a tenant of their home he/she could be guilty of harassment.

Such actions as cutting off services, deliberately allowing the premises to fall into a state of disrepair, or even forcing unwanted sexual attentions, all constitute harassment and a breach of the right to *quiet enjoyment.*

The 1977 Protection from Eviction Act also prohibits the use of violence to gain entry to premises. Even in situations where the landlord has the right to gain entry without a court order it is an offence to use violence.

If entry to the premises is opposed then the landlord should gain a court order.

What can be done against unlawful evictions?
There are two main remedies for unlawful eviction: damages and, as stated above, an injunction.

The injunction
An injunction is an order from the court requiring a person to do, or not to do something. In the case of eviction the court can grant an injunction requiring the landlord to allow a tenant back into occupation of the premises. In the case of harassment an order can

be made preventing the landlord from harassing the tenant. Failure to comply with an injunction is contempt of court and can result in a fine or imprisonment.

Damages

In some cases the tenant can press for *financial compensation* following unlawful eviction. Financial compensation may have to be paid in cases where financial loss has occurred or in cases where personal hardship alone has occurred.

The tenant can also press for *special damages*, which means that the tenant may recover the definable out-of-pocket expenses. These could be expenses arising as a result of having to stay in a hotel because of the eviction. Receipts must be kept in that case. There are also *general damages*, which can be awarded in compensation for stress, suffering and inconvenience.

A tenant may also seek *exemplary damages* where it can be proved that the landlord has disregarded the law deliberately with the intention of making a profit out of the displacement of the tenant.

10

REPAIRS AND IMPROVEMENTS

Repairs and improvements generally: the landlord and tenants obligations

Repairs are essential works to keep the property in good order. Improvements are alterations to the property, e.g. the installation of a shower.

As we have seen, some tenancies are periodic, week-to-week or month-to-month. If a tenancy falls into this category, or is a fixed-term tenancy for less than seven years, and began after October 1961, then a landlord is legally responsible for most major repairs to the flat or house. Repairs are paid for out of your rent.

If a tenancy began after 15th January 1989 then, in addition to the above responsibility, the landlord is also responsible for repairs to common parts and service fittings.

The area of law dealing with the landlord and tenants repairing obligations is the 1985 Landlord and Tenant Act, section 11.

This section of the Act is known as a covenant and cannot be excluded by informal agreement between landlord and tenant. In other words the landlord is legally responsible whether he or she likes it or not. Parties to a tenancy, however, may make an application to a court mutually to vary or exclude this section.

An example of repairs a landlord is responsible for:

Leaking roofs and guttering;
Rotting windows;
Rising damp;
Damp walls;
Faulty electrical wiring;
Dangerous ceilings and staircases;
Faulty gas and water pipes;

Broken water heaters and boilers;
Broken lavatories, sinks or baths.

In shared housing the landlord must see that shared halls, stairways, kitchens and bathrooms are maintained and kept clean and lit.

Normally, tenants are responsible only for minor repairs, e.g., broken door handles, cupboard doors, etc. Tenants will also be responsible for decorations unless they have been damaged as a result of the landlord's failure to do repair.

A landlord will be responsible for repairs only if the repair has been reported. It is therefore important to report repairs in writing and keep a copy. If the repair is not carried out then action can be taken. Damages can also be claimed.

Compensation can be claimed, with the appropriate amount being the reduction in the value of the premises to the tenant caused by the landlord's failure to repair. If the tenant carries out the repairs then the amount expended will represent the decrease in value.

The tenant does not have the right to withhold rent because of a breach of repairing covenant by the landlord. However, depending on the repair, the landlord will not have a very strong case in court if rent is withheld.

REPORTING REPAIRS TO A LANDLORD

The tenant has to tell the landlord or the person collecting the rent straight away when a repair needs doing. It is advisable that it is in writing, listing the repairs that need to be done.

Once a tenant has reported a repair the landlord must do it within a reasonable period of time. What is reasonable will depend on the nature of the repair. If certain emergency work needs to be done by the council, such as leaking guttering or drains a notice can be served ordering the landlord to do the work within a short time. In exceptional cases if a home cannot be made habitable at reasonable cost the council may declare that the house must no longer be used, in which case the council has a legal duty to re-house a tenant.

If after the council has served notice the landlord still does not do the work, the council can send in its own builder or, in some cases take the landlord to court. A tenant must allow a landlord access to do repairs. The landlord has to give twenty-four hours notice of wishing to gain access.

The tenants rights whilst repairs are being carried out

The landlord must ensure that the repairs are done in an orderly and efficient way with minimum inconvenience to the tenant If the works are disruptive or if property or decorations are damaged the tenant can apply to the court for compensation or, if necessary, for an order to make the landlord behave reasonably.

If the landlord genuinely needs the house empty to do the work he/she can ask the tenant to vacate it and can if necessary get a court order against the tenant.

A *written agreement* should be drawn up making it clear that the tenant can move back in when the repairs are completed and stating what the arrangements for fuel charges and rent are.

If a person is an *assured* tenant the landlord could get a court order to make that person give up the home permanently if there is work to be done with him/her in occupation in occupation.

Can the landlord put the rent up after doing repairs?

If there is a service charge for maintenance, the landlord may be able to pass on the cost of the work(s).

Tenants rights to make improvements to a property

Unlike carrying out repairs the tenant will not normally have the right to insist that the landlord make actual alterations to the home. However, a tenant needs the following amenities and the law states that you should have them:

Bath or shower;

Wash hand basin; Hot and cold water at each bath, basin or shower; an indoor toilet.

If these amenities do not exist then the tenant can contact the council's Environmental Health Officer. An improvement notice can be served on the landlord ordering him to put the amenity in.

Disabled tenants

If a tenant is disabled he/she may need special items of equipment in the accommodation. The local authority may help in providing and, occasionally, paying for these. The tenant will need to obtain the permission of the landlord. If you require more information then contact the social services department locally.

Shared housing. The position of tenants in shared houses (Houses in Multiple Occupation)

A major change to improve standards of shared housing was introduced in 2006. The parts of the Housing Act 2004 relating to the licensing of HMO's (Houses in Multiple Occupation) and the new Health and Safety rating System for assessing property conditions came into effect on 6rh April 2006.

The Act requires landlords of many HMO's to apply for licences. The HMO's that need to be licensed are those with:

- Three or more storeys, which are
- Occupied by five or more people forming two or more households (i.e. people not related, living together as a couple etc) and
- Which have an element of shared facilities (eg kitchen, bathroom etc)

As far as licensing is concerned, attics and basements are included as storeys if they are used as living accommodation. Previously, HMO's were only defined as houses converted into flats or bedsits, but the new Act widens this definition and many more types of shared houses are now included.

A local authority will have a list of designated properties will have a list of those properties which are designated HMO's and they will need to be licensed.

Usually, landlords will need to apply to a local authority private sector unit for licences. It has been illegal for landlords to manage designated properties without a licence since July 2006.

Landlords will have to complete an application form and pay a fee, the local authority will then assess whether the property is suitable for the number of people the landlord wants to rent it to. In most case, the local authority, their agents, will visit a property to assess facilities and also fire precautions. A decision will then be taken to grant a license.

There is a fee for registration, councils set the fee and the ones shown below are indicative of a southern local authority:

- Shared houses-five sharers landlords first house £640
- Subsequent house £590
- Plus £10 each additional occupier over five

Hostels

- 10 occupiers £690
- 20 occupiers £790
- 50 occupiers £1100
- 75 occupiers £1340

Housing Grants

There are a range of grants and loans available, almost all discretionary and means tested for help and assistance with property improvement.

Disabled Facilities Grant

The only mandatory grant is the Disabled Facilities Grant, given to those in need, which has been assessed by an Occupational Therapist, the grant has a ceiling. Information of which can be obtained from the local authority. Has the name suggests it is for those who are disabled and are n need of works which will make there property accessible and usable for disabled people.

Disabled Facilities Assistance

Disabled Facilities Assistance is in the form of interest free loans, repayable on disposal of the property. To qualify for DFA a person must be at least 18 years old and a freeholder or leaseholder with at least 10 years to expiry of ease and authority to do the work. The maximum amount of assistance is £25,000 or 50% of the equity existing at the time of application. There are a number of other conditions related to the actual works. Details can be obtained from the local authority.

Decent Homes Loans Assistance

This is available to homeowners to enable them to bring their property up to the national Decent Homes Standard. Homes meet Decent Homes standard if they meet a set of criteria which is laid down by the government, such as thermal insulation, overall state of repair etc. Details of the standards can be obtained from the local authority. There are a number of property related criteria and as the money offered is a loan then it will be means tested.

Common Parts Loan/ Common Parts Assistance

This help and assistance is available to owner occupiers (leaseholders) to assist them to meet their liabilities towards the cost of major refurbishment of the common parts of buildings containing their flats, where one or more of the key components of the common parts are old and require replacement or major repair, leading to one or more of the flats becoming 'non-decent' as defined in government guidance. key components include external walls, roof structure and covering, chimneys etc. Common parts loans are administered by a third party and offered at a subsidised interest rate. They are repayable on disposal of the property. The criteria for Common Part Loans can be obtained from the local authority.

Landlords Major Works Assistance

Local authorities will usually consider assistance to landlords who elect to bring empty properties back into se as accommodation for homeless people. This will involve leasing properties back to the council for a ten-year period. This scheme will depend on the policy of the local authority.

Minor work assistance

Grants are sometimes available to owner-occupiers and tenants for small-scale work for which they have the responsibility. The aim of such grants will be to ensure the person involved achieves the decent homes standard, improves energy efficiency, improves security or to carry out disabled adaptations as an alternative to DFG.

Details of these various grants and the criteria attached to them can be obtained from the local authority.

Energy Innovation Grants

These grants are subject to the availability of funding and are related to the policy of the local authority.

Sanitation health and hygiene

Local authorities have a duty to serve an owner with a notice requiring the provision of WCs when a property has insufficient sanitation, sanitation meaning toilet waste disposal. They will also serve notice if it is thought that the existing sanitation is inadequate and is harmful to health or is a nuisance. Local authorities have similar powers under various Public Health Acts to require owners to put right bad drains and sewers, also food storage facilities and vermin, plus the containing of disease.

The Environmental Health Department, if it considers the problem bad enough will serve a notice requiring the landlord to put the defect right. In certain cases the local authority can actually do the work and require the landlord to pay for it. This is called work *in default*.

11

The Law and Owner Occupiers
COMMONHOLD, FREEHOLD AND LEASEHOLD

Commonhold and Leasehold Reform Act 2002

The Commonhold and Leasehold Reform Act 2002 introduces into English law an entirely new form of tenure, namely commonhold. It is specifically targeted at blocks of flats, where leasehold has been the normal form of tenure until now.

The Government hopes that commonhold will avoid the tensions and conflicts that have sometimes arisen between leaseholders and freeholders. Time will tell whether that hope will be realised. If it is, doubtless commonhold will come to supersede leasehold as the normal form of tenure for premises divided into flats. For the present, however, commonhold and leasehold regimes will operate side by side, with leasehold predominating.

But it would be very reasonable for a flat owner to say at this point, "Wait a minute. Commonhold has been brought in as an alternative to leasehold; but what was wrong with leasehold? And why do I have to trouble myself with all this anyway? Why can't I simply own my flat, the same way as other people own their houses?"

This is a very fair question. To answer it, we need to look at how the law regards property ownership.

Freehold and Leasehold

The law does not look at property in the same way as most lay people. Most people think in terms of houses and other buildings; the law is more interested in the land beneath. A freehold home owner will say "I own my house." But the law will say "He owns the land on which is built the house he lives in." To the law, the key point is that he owns the land - the buildings on it are incidental.

For practical purposes, the strongest form of title to land is that of freeholder. Freehold title lasts forever; it may be bought and sold, or passed by inheritance. In short, freehold title is tantamount to outright ownership, and is taken as such for the purposes of this book.

Freeholders may, of course, use their land for their own purposes. The freehold home owner is merely the most familiar example. But they may also, if they wish, allow other people to use their land. And this is where leases, and other forms of tenure, come in.

Suppose you would like to make use of a piece of land owned by someone else. The owner is unwilling to sell it to you, but, having no immediate use for it himself, is willing to allow you to use it for a time, perhaps in exchange for payment. At its simplest, this arrangement implies no more than a licence - the owner's (i.e. landlord's) permission for you to be on his land.

But such a licence can be revoked by the landlord at any time, with or without a good reason. As such it is not very valuable, so if the owner wants to make money by allowing other people to use his land, he needs to give them a legal status that they will be willing to pay for. This is achieved by granting a lease or tenancy. It should be noted here that, from the legal point of view, a lease and a tenancy are the same thing; but in practice, the terms tend to be used in different contexts. This is explained below: for the present, we shall call it a lease.

A lease grants the leaseholder permission to use the land for a certain period, which can be anything from a day or two to several thousand years. It will usually attach conditions, for example that the leaseholder must pay rent (usually a sum of money, although in principle other goods or services could constitute rent).

The lease may, but does not have to, put certain restrictions on what the leaseholder may do with the land. But it must, in order to be a lease rather than merely a licence, grant the leaseholder 'exclusive possession'. This is the right to exclude other people, especially the landlord, from the land. Such a right need not be absolute, and exceptions to it are explained later in the book: but it is enough to give the leaseholder a high degree of control over the land, which has become, for the duration of the lease, very much the leaseholder's land rather than the freeholder's. A lease, unless it contains a stipulation to the contrary, may be bought, sold, or inherited; if this happens, all the rights and duties under it pass to the new owner.

Leases and Tenancies

Confusion is often caused by the fact that, although the terms leaseholder (or lessee) and tenant are legally interchangeable, they tend to be used in different senses. The tendency is to refer to short leases as tenancies: the more substantial the rights conferred, and the longer the period for which they run, the likelier it is that the agreement will be referred to as a lease. For the purposes of this book, an agreement will be referred to as a 'tenancy' if it is periodic or runs for a fixed term of less than seven years. A fixed term agreement running for more than seven years will be referred to as a 'lease'.

A 'periodic' tenancy is one that runs from period to period (usually, from week to week or month to month) until something intervenes to stop it, and is conditional on payment of rent. A tenancy that runs for a fixed term of less than seven years has a definite date of expiry but is otherwise similar to a periodic tenancy and will depend on regular payment of rent. Tenancies granted by local authorities and housing associations tend to be periodic; private landlords generally grant either periodic tenancies or short fixed-term tenancies (typically, six months). At any rate, the landlord of a periodic or short-term tenancy will usually accept most of the responsibility for maintaining the property and will charge a relatively high rent to allow for this. If the tenancy is for residential property, the landlord's duty to maintain the dwelling is imposed by law (Landlord and Tenant Act 1985).

It is common for private landlords to insist on prepayment of rent or a deposit before granting a tenancy, and many landlords will levy a separate service charge to cover the cost of some activities that are peripheral to the central one of providing housing; but despite these costs it would be true to say that the principal financial responsibility accepted by a periodic or short-term tenant is that of paying the rent. The position of a leaseholder is very different. The major financial commitment will usually be a substantial initial payment either to the landlord (if the lease is newly created) or to the previous leaseholder. There is still a rent, called a ground rent, payable to the landlord, but it is usually a notional amount (£50 or £100 a year is not uncommon). Its purpose is not so much to give the landlord an income as to give the leaseholder an annual reminder that ultimate ownership of the land is not his.

Types of Leasehold Property
In the context of residential property, it should be noted that the great majority of leases relate to flats rather than houses. This is because of the legal concept of land tenure as described above. If a builder buys some freehold land and covers it in houses, it is possible to parcel out the area so that each bit of freehold land, and the house standing on it, can be sold separately. It does not matter if the houses are semi-detached or terraced, because there is well-established law governing party walls of adjoining freeholders. But if there are flats, the builder has a problem: how can the flats be sold since they cannot be said to stand on separate and distinct bits of land? The answer is to sell leases.

Where flats are sold, each purchaser acquires a lease that gives him specified rights over the parcel of land on which the flats stand. These rights, of course, are shared by the leaseholders of the other flats. In addition, however, each leaseholder gains the right to exclusive possession of part of the building occupying the land - his own flat. The leaseholder would say "I own my flat", but the law says "He owns a lease granting him certain rights, in particular that of access, to a defined parcel of land and the right of exclusive possession of specified parts of a building erected on that land." This may seem a slightly unusual way of looking at it, but it is fundamental to understanding the way that the law sees the relationship between leaseholders of flats and their freeholders.

The freehold of flatted property will often be retained by the developer, although sometimes it will be sold to a property company. Formerly, it was common practice for the freehold to be retained even when separate houses were built. This allowed the freeholder to retain an interest in the property and, above all, to regain full possession of it when the lease expired. However, the position of freeholders has been weakened by three key pieces of legislation, the Leasehold Reform Act 1967, the Leasehold Reform, Housing and Urban Development Act 1993, and the Commonhold and Leasehold Reform Act 2002. These Acts are described in detail in Chapter Four: their overall effect is to entitle leaseholders either to the freehold of houses or to a new lease of flats. In view of the legislation, there is now little point in the original owner's attempting to retain the freehold of land on which houses have been built. The exception is where a house is sold on the basis of shared ownership - see below.

Most residential leasehold property therefore consists of flats. Of these, most are in the private sector, comprising purpose-built blocks and (especially in London) conversions of what were once large single houses. The freehold will usually belong to the developer, to a property company, or sometimes to the original owner of the site.

House leases normally give most of the repairing responsibility to the leaseholder - services provided by the freeholder, and therefore service charges, are minimal. In flats, however, although the leaseholder will normally be responsible for the interior of the flat, the freeholder will maintain the fabric of the building and will recoup the costs of doing so by levying service charges on the leaseholders. This is an area of such potential conflict between leaseholders and freeholders that it has been the subject of legislation. It is dealt with fully in Chapter Three.

Mixed-tenure blocks: the right to buy
The general shift from renting to owning means that sometimes flats have been sold in blocks that were originally developed for letting to tenants: the result is often a 'mixed-tenure' block, with both leaseholders and tenants. Although this sometimes happens in the private sector, it is particularly common in blocks owned by local authorities and housing associations, for it is to these that the statutory right to buy applies. This right was created by the Housing Act 1980 and allows most local authority tenants, and some housing

association tenants, to buy their homes at a heavily discounted price. Tenants of houses are normally sold the freehold, but tenants of flats become leaseholders.

The right to buy, often seen as the flagship policy of Margaret Thatcher's government, was bitterly opposed, because of the loss it involves of homes otherwise available for letting to the needy and because its popularity with council tenants called into question their previously solid electoral support for Labour. On both counts, its critics' fears have to some extent been realised; however, the right to buy has become an increasingly accepted feature of local authority housing. More recently, a similar but less generous scheme has been introduced covering many housing association tenants not already qualifying for the full right to buy. Purchasing a council home has been, for most of the million or so that have done so, a very satisfactory investment. A minority of purchasers have, however, met with serious difficulties, particularly where they have become leaseholders in mixed tenure blocks of flats: Chapter Three looks at some of the problems affecting management and service charges.

Shared ownership

Another result of the trend towards home ownership has been the dramatic expansion of shared ownership. This is a form of tenure that combines leasing and renting. However, the term 'shared ownership' is something of a misnomer because ownership is not, in fact, shared between the leaseholder and the freeholder. The lease relates to the whole property, not part of it, and the shared owner is as entitled as any other leaseholder to consider himself the owner of his house. The key point about shared ownership leases is not that they give an inferior form of tenure to other leases but that they have different conditions attached. The leaseholder pays less than the full value of the lease; typically, half. In exchange for this concession, he pays not the normal notional ground rent but a much more substantial rent. However, he is much more a leaseholder than he is a tenant, and, like other leaseholders (but unlike tenants) is responsible for the internal repair of the property and, in the case of houses, usually the fabric of the building too.

Shared owners usually have the right to increase their stake as and when they can afford it: this is called 'staircasing' because the owner's share goes up in steps. If the property is a house, the freehold will normally be transferred when the owner's share reaches 100%, and he will then be in the same position as any other freehold home owner. If it is a flat, he will continue to be a leaseholder but there will no longer be a rental (other than ground rent).

Head leases and Subleases

For the sake of clarity and brevity, this book has been written throughout on the basis that there are only two parties involved: the freeholder and the leaseholder. Usually this picture is accurate; but it is the right of the leaseholder, unless the lease specifically forbids it, to sublet the property, or part of it, to someone else. This means that the leaseholder delegates some of his rights over the property to another person. Obviously, he cannot delegate rights greater than his own, so that if he holds a lease of the property running until 2025 he cannot grant a sublease running until 2050. And he cannot grant a sublease of the whole of his rights because this would leave him with no interest in the property: it would, in fact, amount to the same as an assignment (see Chapter Two). So it is necessary for a sublease that the original leaseholder be left with something; either some period of time or some part of the property.

It is possible in theory to have a whole hierarchy of leases applying to a particular property, starting with the freehold, then the head lease, then a sublease, followed by sub-subleases and possibly sub-sub-subleases below those. There are two rules that limit this kind of proliferation: one, explained above, is that each lease must confer less, in space or time or both, than the one above it; and the other, that if a lease may not be held by the same person as hold the lease (or freehold) immediately above it.

Even with these limitations, however, long chains of ownership can develop. Suppose I own the freehold of a certain piece of land. I am unwilling to sell it outright but I agree to lease it for 125 years to a property developer to build flats, so he becomes the head leaseholder and leases the flats for 99 years to individual subleaseholders. One of these leases his flat for 25 years to someone that, in turn, lets it on a tenancy. The tenant then sublets to some other person who (remembering that tenancies and leases are legally the same) thus becomes a sub-sub-sub-subleaseholder (if I have counted correctly). And it is possible to devise even taller hierarchies of lease than this, provided always that no one holds a lease from himself and that each lease grants less, even if only slightly, than the one above it.

Commonhold

To try to deal with problems arising from the relationship between freeholders and leaseholders, a new form of tenure, 'commonhold', was created by the Commonhold and Leasehold Reform Act 2002. It is designed specifically for use in blocks of flats, and the idea is that all the individual flat owners (or 'unit holders', as the Act calls them) will belong to a 'commonhold association', a registered company that operate under a constitution (the 'memorandum and articles') and act in accordance with a 'commonhold community statement'.

This arrangement ensures that each unit holder will have two separate interests in relation to the property: individually, in his own particular unit, and collectively, in the block as a whole.

12

OBLIGATIONS OF FREEHOLDER AND LEASEHOLDER

General Principles

For centuries the law did little to regulate the relationship between freeholders and leaseholders. The view was taken that they had entered into the relationship of their own free will, and it was up to them to agree whatever terms and conditions they liked. If either party did not keep the bargain, he could of course be sued in the courts, but, on the whole, the law did not interfere in the bargain itself.

In the twentieth century, however, the view grew up that some types of bargain are inherently unfair and even those that are not might still be open to exploitation.

An example of the first type is an agreement that residential property will revert to the original freeholder at the end of a long lease. This meant that when 99-year leases expired, leaseholders found that their homes had abruptly returned to the outright ownership of the heir of the original freeholder, leaving them as mere trespassers liable to be ejected at any time. In practice, freeholders were usually willing to grant a fresh lease, but sometimes only at a very high price that the leaseholder might well be unable to afford. In some cases, freeholders insisted on reclaiming the property however much the leaseholder offered, and the law supported them. This is the state of affairs that led to legislation entitling almost all residential leaseholders to extend their leases, and many of them to claim the freehold. This is dealt with in Chapter Four.

The freeholder's right to demand a service charge is an example of an arrangement that is fair in principle but open to abuse in practice. It is inevitable, especially in flats, that responsibility for some types of repair cannot be ascribed to any individual leaseholder and must therefore be retained by the freeholder; who must, in turn, recoup the cost from leaseholders. However, some freeholders abused this system by levying extravagant service charges that made the service charge a source of profit. To prevent this, there is now a substantial body of legislation designed to ensure that freeholders carry out only the works that are really necessary and that they recover their legitimate costs and no more. The complicated rules governing this are chiefly found in the Landlord and Tenant Act 1985 (as amended) and are described in Chapter Three.

Under the Landlord and Tenant Act 1987, either party to a long lease (one originally granted for at least 21 years) may go to the Leasehold Valuation Tribunal (or 'LVT') to argue that the lease is deficient in some way and needs to be changed. If only the one lease is affected, the tribunal may vary it. Sometimes, however, a number of leases may need to be changed; in this case either the freeholder or 75% of the leaseholders may apply.

Obligations of Leaseholders

The obligations of leaseholders are set out in the lease; indeed, since it is a document drafted by or on behalf of freeholders, one of its main aims is to tell leaseholders what they must and must not do. However, legislation and judicial decisions sometimes come to the leaseholder's assistance.

Consumer legislation can also apply to leases; in particular, the Unfair Terms in Consumer Contracts Regulations 1999 (which replace earlier regulations made in 1995) have a major impact. These apply to standard terms in contracts. This means they normally cover the terms of leases, which are usually presented to potential leaseholders as a package with no opportunity to renegotiate individual terms. Occasionally, however, individual terms can be specifically negotiated and it should be noted that in that case the Unfair Terms Regulations do not apply. Nor will they apply to any lease granted before the earlier version of the regulations came in in July 1995. The Office of Fair Trading has issued advice about the types of term that are likely to be judged unfair in the context of assured tenancies.

The OFT has not issued advice about long leases, but it is likely that similar standards would apply.

a: *Plain and intelligible language*

Over many years property lawyers have developed an obscure and technical language that can have the effect of excluding outsiders. This form of 'legalese' is characterised by unwieldy sentences with few (or no) commas to break them up, long lists often consisting of different names for the same thing, and a vocabulary of unfamiliar words and (worst of all) familiar words given unfamiliar meanings.

For instance, in normal English the verb 'determine' means 'ascertain' or 'firmly decide', but when a property lawyer applies it to a lease it means 'end' or 'terminate' (as in 'the lease shall determine if...'). Property lawyers also have a well-merited reputation for using words like 'hereinafter' and 'aforesaid', which, although not ambiguous, are hardly everyday English, while occasional outbreaks of Latin are not unknown (*pari passu* and *mutatis mutandis*).

Thankfully, this style is going out of fashion and an increasing number of modern leases are being written in more intelligible language, and for leases made since 1995 the Unfair Terms Regulations mean that arcanely written terms may be unenforceable. However, a huge number of leases written in traditional style still have decades or even centuries to run, so unfortunately property lawyers' English will be with us for a long time yet.

b: *Terms Unfair on Consumers*

There are some terms to which the Office of Fair Trading objects in any consumer contract. These are terms that place an unreasonable burden on the customer (the leaseholder) or give an unfair advantage to the supplier (the freeholder). Some of these terms are common in long leases.

There may be a clause in which the leaseholder declares that he has 'read and understood' the lease, even though the document is long and complex and it unlikely that anyone would read (or understand) the whole of it. The aim is to put the leaseholder at a disadvantage in any dispute by arguing that he was fully aware of all the terms of the lease. Another way of loading the scales is a clause allowing the freeholder the final decision about vital matters, such as whether or not the freeholder and the leaseholder have fulfilled their respective obligations under the lease.

These clauses are probably unenforceable in leases made since July 1995, but in earlier leases they are probably valid.

There are other types of clause that are potentially a problem for the leaseholder. An example is a clause laying down procedural formalities. Such a clause is not necessarily a problem: for instance, leases commonly require formal communications between the freeholder and the leaseholder to be in writing, and this is a perfectly reasonable requirement because it reduces the chances misunderstandings or disputes about who said what. But it is harder to justify a requirement for notices to be sent by registered post, and some leases stipulate procedures that are so onerous that the aim seems to be to deter leaseholders from exercising their rights.

Similar comments apply to clauses imposing financial penalties for breaches of the lease. This is not necessarily unreasonable, but sometimes the penalties are out of all proportion to the nature of the breach.

Some leases require the leaseholder to join with the freeholder (and help with the cost) in responding to legal or other notices pertaining to the property. Again, this may be reasonable in some circumstances, but as a blanket requirement it can act against leaseholders' interests.

An interesting and debatable issue is the prohibition of set-off, which is a standard clause in most leases. 'Set-off' is the practice of deducting (or 'setting off') from any payment made by one party under an agreement any sums that are owed by the other party. For instance, suppose a leaseholder considers that a repair to the fabric of the building is the freeholder's responsibility, but the freeholder either disputes this or fails to take any action. Eventually the leaseholder does the work at his own expense, and next time the annual service charge falls due he reimburses himself by deducting, or 'setting off', the cost from his service charge payment.

Leaseholders like set-off because it is an easy way of reclaiming disputed sums from the freeholder, and it shifts onto the freeholder the onus of continuing the dispute. Freeholders dislike it for exactly the same reasons, which is why leases normally prohibit it. The Office of Fair Trading, in its advice on assured tenancies, says that prohibiting set-off is unfair, but it is not clear whether the same advice would apply to leases.

The possibility that unfair, or potentially unfair, clauses will feature in a lease underlines the need for competent legal advice before signing it. An experienced solicitor will be able to advise whether doubtful clauses can be, or are likely to be, used against leaseholders. Leaseholders may also have remedies available under the Landlord and Tenant Act: this is covered below and, in the key area of service charges, in the next Chapter.

c: Restrictive clauses in leases

So far, we have looked at leases as if they were consumer contracts, and outlined some of the clauses they may contain that could affect leaseholders in their capacity as consumers. But there are some further potentially difficult terms that relate specifically to property issues. These terms are not necessarily unreasonable. For example, in a lease concerning an upstairs flat it would be quite normal to have a clause requiring the leaseholder to keep the premises carpeted. This makes sense because bare floors, although currently very fashionable, could be very noisy for the people in the flat below.

The Office of Fair Trading's advice identifies several types of sweeping provisions that would, if they were enforced, considerably restrict the tenant's ability to live a normal life. Although the OFT's advice relates to assured tenancies, similar objections would probably apply to these clauses in leases. For example:

- **Pets** Leases often lay down that the leaseholder may not own pets, or may not do so without the freeholder's permission.
- **Upkeep** Leases may say that the leaseholder must decorate periodically - say, every five or seven years. Where there is a garden, it is common for the leaseholder to be required to keep it in good order.
- **Business** Leases often lay down that the leaseholder must not run any sort of business from his home.

96

- **Use as residence** A lease will generally say that the property is to be used for the residential purposes of the leaseholder and his household, and that it cannot be sublet. It will sometimes attempt to restrict how many people may live there apart from the leaseholder.
- **Other** Leases sometimes forbid such things as the keeping of flammable materials and the installation of television aerials or satellite dishes. They may require leaseholders to drain hot water systems whenever they are away, or keep the premises clean and free of dust.

It is easy to see why freeholders want such clauses in the lease: it is because they realise that there will be serious problems if someone attempts, for instance, to keep four alsatians in a studio flat. The neighbours will be inconvenienced and will complain to the freeholder, and leases of other flats in the same block will become difficult to sell.

The same arguments could apply if one of the leaseholders allows his flat to fall into complete decorative decay or if he runs a noisy and busy trade from his home.

But the kind of blanket rules that appear in many leases go too far. A rule against any pets at all forbids not only four noisy alsatians but also entirely inoffensive pets such as a budgie or a goldfish. In the same way, prohibiting business activities means that the leaseholder may not use his home to write a book for publication, or address envelopes, and so on - types of homeworking that could not possibly inconvenience anyone.

The rule against sub-letting also prevents leaseholders from exploiting the value of their property by letting it out, something that is open to most home-owners and is increasingly accepted as normal.

For leases made since July 1995, these sweeping clauses are probably unfair and unenforceable. But even for older leases, the reality is that such broad provisions are seldom enforced. Freeholders, and their lawyers, like them because they feel that they preserve their freedom of action, allowing them to decide whether or not to enforce the lease if it is clear that one of these blanket conditions is being broken. But there are two problems with this attitude.

The first is that it creates uncertainty in the minds of leaseholders. Suppose the leases in a block of flats prohibit all pets, but leaseholder A has a goldfish and no action has been taken even though the freeholder is aware of the infringement. Leaseholder B may well conclude that there will be no objection if he gets a cat. If still there is no action, leaseholder C may feel able to get a couple of dogs - and so on. So the fact that restrictions are so broad can have the paradoxical effect of reducing their effectiveness.

The second problem is that if, in the example just given, the freeholder takes legal action to force C to get rid of the dogs, it is possible that C will argue in court that the treatment of the other leaseholders shows that the freeholder is not seriously interested in banning pets and that the action has been motivated rather by petty spite or bias.

It would be better if freeholders and their lawyers drafted leases that say what they mean: not that leaseholders may have no pets at all, but that they may have no pets apt to damage the property or cause inconvenience or annoyance to other persons. The same principle should apply to clauses dealing with sub-letting or working from home.

It is unfortunate that this book is forced to advise leaseholders to ignore some parts of their leases. The responsibility for this, however, lies with freeholders and their lawyers for writing into standard leases blanket conditions purporting to prohibit entirely inoffensive behaviour. This practice makes it inevitable, in the real world, that leaseholders will disregard certain clauses, and that books like this will have to give them some indication of when they can probably do so safely. Most leaseholders exercise common sense and realise that the freeholder is unlikely to take action unless there is a complaint, which means that the leaseholder may do almost whatever he pleases provided he refrains from provoking anyone. It is sensible to stay on good terms with neighbours to ensure that if anything is bothering them they take it up directly with you rather than report the matter to the freeholder. Other leaseholders will also be able to tell you what view has been taken in the past - both by other residents and by the freeholder - in doubtful cases.

d: Restrictions on sale

Some leases restrict the kind of person to whom the lease may be sold (or 'assigned' - see below). For example, a housing scheme may have been intended specifically for the elderly. Clearly, it will not be maintained as such if leaseholders are free to assign or bequeath their leases to whomever they please, so the lease will say that it may be assigned only to persons above a certain age, and that if it is inherited by anyone outside the age group it must be sold on to someone qualified to hold it. Although this could be described as an onerous term because it makes it more difficult to find a buyer and may reduce the lease's value, it is reasonable given the need to ensure that the scheme continues to house elderly people exclusively. And the restriction it imposes is not too severe because so many potential purchasers qualify.

However, some leases define much more narrowly to whom they may be sold. Sometimes the freeholder is a body owned and run by the leaseholders themselves, and in these cases it is usual to require that all leaseholders must join the organisation and, if they leave it, must immediately dispose of the lease to someone that is willing to join. Again, such a term is not necessarily unacceptable. If the organisation makes relatively light demands on its members (perhaps no more than a modest admission fee or annual subscription), the restriction is unlikely greatly to diminish the value of the lease. If, however, the organisation expects much more from its members - perhaps that they actively take part in running it, or that they pay a large annual subscription - the value of the lease will be severely reduced because it will be difficult to find purchasers willing to accept the conditions. A key point is whether the organisation has power to expel members, thus forcing them to sell; and, if so, in what circumstances and by whom this power can be exercised.

e: Access

Virtually any lease will contain a clause allowing the freeholder to enter the property in order to inspect or repair it. This has the effect of qualifying the leaseholder's right of exclusive possession (see below), but only subject to certain conditions. The freeholder (or the freeholder's servants, such as agents or contractors) may enter only at reasonable times, and subject to the giving of reasonable notice. If these conditions are not met, the leaseholder is under no obligation to allow them in; and, even when the conditions are met, the landlord will be trespassing if he enters the property without the leaseholder's consent. If the leaseholder refuses consent even though the time is reasonable and reasonable notice has been given, the landlord's remedy is to get a court order against the leaseholder compelling him to grant entry. It is probable, in such a case, that the landlord will seek, and get, an award of legal costs against the leaseholder.

f: Arbitration

Many leases contain clauses providing that disputes can be submitted to arbitration at the request of either party. By the Commonhold and Leasehold Reform Act, the effect of these clauses is limited, because the results will not be binding so far as the Leasehold Valuation Tribunal is concerned. If, however, once a dispute has arisen, the parties to agree to submit it to an agreed arbitrator, they are bound by the result, which is enforceable by the courts. If such a 'post-dispute' arbitration finds that the leaseholder is in breach, this is equivalent to a finding by the LVT and will (if the other requirements are met) allow the freeholder to proceed with forfeiture. Arbitration may be a useful mechanism in some cases, and it may be cheaper and quicker than legal action, but it may be difficult to find an arbitrator in whom both parties have confidence.

Obligations of Freeholders
a: Exclusive possession *and quiet enjoyment*
The first and most important obligation on the freeholder, without which there would be no legal lease at all, is to respect the leaseholder's rights of 'exclusive possession' and 'quiet enjoyment'. Exclusive possession has been explained in Chapter One as the

right to occupy the property and exclude others from it, especially the freeholder. Quiet enjoyment is another way of underlining the leaseholder's rights over the property: it means that the freeholder may not interfere with the leaseholder's use of the property provided that the terms of the lease are observed.

However, the leaseholder's right to quiet enjoyment applies only to breaches by the freeholder or the freeholder's servants such as agents or contractors. It is important to note this because the term is sometimes thought to mean that the freeholder must protect the leaseholder against any activity by anyone that interferes with his use of the property: this is not so. For example, if the freeholder carries out some activity elsewhere in the building that interferes with the leaseholder, the leaseholder's right to quiet enjoyment has been breached and he is entitled to redress unless the freeholder can show that the activity was necessary, for instance to comply with repairing obligations under the lease. But if the interference is caused by someone else, perhaps another leaseholder, the freeholder's obligation to provide quiet enjoyment has not been breached. And it is worth stressing in this connection that even if the other leaseholder is in breach of his lease, it is entirely up to the freeholder whether or not to take action: other leaseholders have no power to force the freeholder to deal with the situation.

This means that if one leaseholder is breaking his lease by holding noisy parties late at night, the other leaseholders may ask, but may not require, the freeholder to take action to enforce the lease. They may, however, take legal action directly against the offending leaseholder for nuisance.

b: The Section 48 notice
Another important protection for leaseholders is found in section 48 of the Landlord and Tenant Act 1987. This was designed to deal with the situation in which freeholders seek to avoid their responsibilities by (to put it bluntly) doing a disappearing act. Sometimes freeholders would provide no address or telephone number or other means of contact, meaning that leaseholders were unable to hold the freeholder to his side of the agreement. Sections 47 and 48 therefore lay down that the freeholder must formally

notify the leaseholder of his name and give an address within England and Wales at which he can be contacted, and that this information must be repeated on every demand for rent or service charge. This has proved especially valuable for leaseholders where the freeholder lives abroad, or is a company based abroad. It should be noted that the address does not have to be the freeholder's home, nor, if the freeholder is a company, its registered office; often it will be the address of a solicitor or property management company, or simply an accommodation address. But the key point is that any notice, or legal writ, is validly served if sent to that address, and the freeholder is not allowed to claim that it never came to his notice.

It is not necessary for the notice required by section 48 to be given in a separate document; it is enough if the name and address is clearly given as part of some other document such as a service charge demand. But if the necessary notice is **not** given, no payment of rent, service charge, or anything else is due to the freeholder; the leaseholder may lawfully withhold it until section 48 is complied with. But leaseholders withholding payments on this ground must be careful; once the notice is given, it has retrospective effect, so that all the money due to the freeholder then becomes due immediately. Any leaseholder withholding money on the grounds that section 48 has not been complied with should, therefore, make sure that he has the money easily available so that he can pay up if he has to.

c: Good management
The freeholder is under an obligation to ensure that his management responsibilities are carried out in a proper and appropriate way. Leaseholders can challenge the freeholder in court or at the LVT if they believe they can show that they are not receiving the standard of management to which they are entitled. This may be an expensive and lengthy process but it better than the alternative, sometimes resorted to by leaseholders, of withholding rent or service charge. This is risky because, whatever the shortcomings of the freeholder's management, it puts the leaseholders in breach of the conditions of their lease and, as such,

demonstrably in the wrong (even if the freeholder may be in the wrong as well).

Withholding due payments is therefore not recommended unless the freeholder is so clearly at fault that arguably no payment is due - for instance, if the service being charged for has clearly not been provided at all (as opposed to being provided inadequately), or if there has been no 'section 48' notice (see above). If leaseholders choose to withhold payment, they are strongly advised to keep the money readily to hand so that they can pay up at once if the freeholder rectifies the problem; the danger otherwise is that they will be taken to court and required to pay immediately to avoid forfeiture (see below).

Powers of Leaseholders over Management

If leaseholders want a scrutiny of the standards of management of their flats, they have power under the Leasehold Reform, Housing and Urban Development Act 1993 to demand a management audit by an auditor acting on behalf of at least two-thirds of the qualifying leaseholders. Qualifying leaseholders are those with leases of residential property originally granted for 21 years or more and requiring them to contribute to the cost of services.

The purpose of the audit, the costs of which must be met by the leaseholders demanding it, is to discover whether the freeholder's duties are being carried out efficiently and effectively. The auditor is appointed by the leaseholders and must be either a qualified accountant or a qualified surveyor and must not live in the block concerned. The auditor has the right to demand papers from the freeholder and can go to court if they are not produced.

Leaseholders' Right to Manage

Leaseholders with long leases (those originally granted for 21 years or more) also have the right to take over management of their block if they wish. This applies to blocks of two or more flats (five or more if there is a resident landlord) and no substantial non-residential part. It does not apply if the freeholder is a local authority.

The leaseholders must first form a 'Right to Manage' company

('RtM' company), which is a limited company whose membership is confined to leaseholders and the freeholder. Before seeking to take over management the RtM company must advise all leaseholders of its intention and invite them to participate. Fourteen days after this invitation, and provided the RtM company includes at least half the eligible tenants (or both, if only two are eligible), it can serve a claim notice on the landlord (or on the Leasehold Valuation Tribunal, if the landlord is untraceable) giving at least four months' notice of its intention to take over the management. The landlord has a month to serve a counter-notice objecting to the claim, in which case the LVT will adjudicate. If no counter-notice is served, or if the LVT so decides, the RtM company duly takes over management.

The landlord must bring to an end as quickly as possible any existing management arrangements applying to the block. The RtM company takes over the landlord's management functions, including services, repairs, maintenance, improvements, and insurance. The landlord retains its role in respect of any flats without long leaseholders (for example, those let on assured tenancies), and continues to deal with forfeiture (for more on forfeiture see the section below 'If the lease is breached'). Essentially the RtM company steps into the landlord's shoes so far as management is concerned, and it is responsible to both the landlord and the individual leaseholders for the proper carrying out of its functions.

Many leases require the landlord's approval before certain things can be done, such as assigning the lease or sub-letting. The RtM company takes over this function from the landlord, but must consult the landlord before granting approval. If the landlord objects, the matter is referred to the LVT. It seems, however, that refusal of consent by the RtM is final and cannot be challenged by the landlord (although it might be challenged by the leaseholder in question on the ground that the relevant term of the lease is unenforceable). The RtM company has authority to enforce covenants in the lease, but not by means of forfeiture. At first blush the power to take over management in this way may appear attractive. However, leaseholders should think very carefully before they commit themselves; there are some potential snags.

The biggest problem is one of enforcement. So long as all

leaseholders are agreed about what needs to be done, and are all willing and able to meet their obligations (including that of paying for services), enforcement will not be an issue and all will be well. But if some individual leaseholders refuse to pay their share, or fail to abide by the covenants in their leases, the RtM company will have to act to enforce the leases and this may well be difficult. In the first place, any steps to enforce leases will pit neighbour against neighbour and are virtually certain to cause animosity in the block. Secondly, the powerful tool of forfeiture, or threatened forfeiture, is denied to a RtM company. Finally, the RtM company, unlike most freeholders, will not have any substantial financial resources that would allow it to pursue lengthy legal action against individual leaseholders.

There are other issues. The RtM company will depend on the voluntary efforts of its members, and experience shows that many people are not willing to put in the time and effort involved in attending meetings and carrying out essential administration. RtM companies have to operate under a special constitution laid down by the Government; the aim of this is to guarantee all leaseholders' rights to be involved, but because the constitution is a standard document applying to all cases it is likely that many leaseholders will find it clumsy and inflexible. Finally, there is the question of continuing relations with the freeholder, which will expect its interests as ultimate owner to be respected by the RtM company.

In short, leaseholders contemplating the formation of a RtM company need to be sure that they are committed not only for the immediate effort of setting it up but for the long haul of carrying out management in the future. They should also recognise that, no matter how united everyone may be to start with, sooner or later the issue of enforcement will rear its head. They should certainly get legal advice about their new responsibilities before committing themselves.

The law allows another remedy in extreme cases of mismanagement. A leaseholder can use the Landlord and Tenant Act 1987 to force the appointment of a managing agent to run the block instead of the freeholder. The leaseholder must serve a notice telling the freeholder what the problems are and warning that unless they are put right a Leasehold Valuation Tribunal will be asked to appoint a managing agent. The LVT may make such an order if it satisfied that it is 'just and convenient'; the Act mentions, as specific examples where this may apply, cases where the freeholder is in breach of obligations under the lease and cases where service charges are being levied in respect of work of a poor standard or an unnecessarily high standard. It should be noted that this procedure, although in some ways it resembles the procedures for collective enfranchisement in Chapter Five, differs from them in that it can be carried out by any individual leaseholder; it does not require the consent of a majority. Note too that the procedure is not available if the freeholder is a local authority, a registered housing association, or the Crown.

Recognised Tenants' Association

A recognised tenants' association (RTA), where there is one, has additional rights to be consulted about managing agents. The RTA can serve a notice requiring the freeholder to supply details of the managing agent and the terms of the management agreement. Recognised tenants' associations are more important, however, in connexion with service charges, so they are explained in the Chapter Three.

Leaseholders that are receiving a consistently poor or overpriced service may also wish to consider getting rid of the freeholder altogether by collective enfranchisement under the Leasehold Reform, Housing and Urban Development Act 1993.

Assignment of Leases

One of the most important characteristics of a lease - in marked contrast to most tenancies - is that it may be bought and sold. Usually, the freeholder has no say in this: the leaseholder may sell to whom he likes for the best price he can get, provided that the purchaser agrees to be bound by the terms of the lease. It is, however, usual for the lease to lay down that the freeholder must be informed of any change of leaseholder.

What actually happens when a lease is sold is that the vendor agrees to transfer to the buyer his rights and obligations under the lease. This is called 'assignment' of the lease. In some types of housing the freeholder has the right to intervene if an assignment is envisaged. The housing may, for instance, be reserved for a particular category of resident, such as the retired, so the freeholder is allowed to refuse consent to the assignment if the purchaser does not qualify.

It was mentioned above that the assignee takes over all the rights and responsibilities attaching to the lease. This means, for instance, that he takes responsibility for any arrears of service charge. This is why purchasers' solicitors go to such lengths to ensure that no arrears or other unusual obligations are outstanding.

If the Lease Is Breached

If the terms of a lease are broken, the party offended against can go to court. This may be the leaseholder, for instance if the freeholder has failed to carry out a repair. But it is normally the freeholder that takes the leaseholder to court, for failure to pay ground rent or service charges or for breach of some other requirement.

It is for the court, if satisfied that the lease has been breached, to decide what to do. The normal remedy will be that the offending party must pay compensation and that the breach (if it is still continuing) must be put right. It is also likely that the loser will be obliged to pay the winner's legal costs as well as his own, a penalty often considerably more severe that the requirement to pay compensation.

A much more severe remedy open to the freeholder if the leaseholder is in breach is forfeiture of the lease. This means what it says: the lease is forfeit to the freeholder. Forfeiture is sometimes threatened by the more aggressive class of freeholder but the good news for leaseholders is that in practice courts have shown themselves loth to grant it except in very serious cases. Since the Housing Act 1996 took effect, forfeiture for unpaid service charges has been made more difficult for freeholders; this is covered in the next Chapter.

Where forfeiture is threatened for any reason other than failure to pay rent (which, depending on the terms of the lease, may or may not include the service charge element), the freeholder must first serve a 'section 146 notice', so called after the relevant provision of the Law of Property Act 1925. In this he must state the nature of the breach of the lease, what action is required to put it right; if he wants monetary compensation for the breach, the notice must state this too.

Before the section 146 notice can be issued, it must be established that a breach of the lease has occurred. If the leaseholder has admitted the breach, the notice can be issued; otherwise, it must have been decided by a court, the LVT, or an independent arbitrator that the leaseholder is in breach. Moreover, the breach of the lease specified in the section 146 notice must have occurred during the twelve years preceding the notice. For breaches older than this, no valid section 146 notice can be served and so forfeiture is not available.

If the notice is not complied with, the freeholder may proceed to forfeit; but the leaseholder may go to court for relief from forfeiture. In practice, courts have generally been willing to grant relief, but they cannot do so unless it is formally applied for. If the leaseholder, perhaps failing to realise the seriousness of the situation, fails to go to court and seek relief, the forfeiture will go ahead.

Forfeiture will be considered again in the next Chapter, which covers the special rules applying to forfeiture for failure to pay service charges.

The Government has announced that ultimately it intends to replace forfeiture by a different remedy that will recognise the value of the leaseholder's interest. Until this happens, however, forfeiture remains available and leaseholders must take care to avoid any possibility of its being used against them.

If the freeholder breaches the lease, the leaseholder can go to court and seek an order requiring the freeholder to remedy the breach, to pay damages, or to do both. The commonest type of breach complained of by leaseholders is failure to carry out repairs, and this explains why action by leaseholders is less usual; they know that if they force the freeholder to do repairs the costs will be recovered through service charges. Legal action may be the best course if the dispute affects a single leaseholder; but if a number of leaseholders are involved they may well prefer to get rid of the freeholder altogether by collectively enfranchising their leases as described in Chapter Four.

Leasehold Valuation Tribunals

Several references have already been made to Leasehold Valuation Tribunals. These bodies operate throughout England and Wales. They are appointed jointly by the Lord Chancellor and (in England) the Environment Secretary and (in Wales) the Welsh Secretary. They perform a large number of quasi-judicial functions in relation to property, especially leasehold property, and feature frequently in this book.

13

OWNER OCCUPIERS AND SERVICE CHARGES

The Role of Service Charges

By far the commonest cause of dispute between leaseholders and freeholders is the provision of services and, especially, the levying of service charges. In extreme cases, leaseholders have been asked to contribute thousands of pounds towards the cost of major repairs, and have even suffered forfeiture of the lease if they are unable, or unwilling, to comply. Happily, such instances are rare; but even where the service charges are more moderate, they are often resented by leaseholders. The purpose of this Chapter is to explain the legitimate purpose of service charges and the legal obligations of both the leaseholder and the freeholder, and to offer some warnings about the circumstances where very high service charges are likely to be found.

The difference between long leases and tenancies (short-term and periodic) has been set out in previous chapters. One of its most important consequences is that services are paid for in a very different way. In a periodic or short-term tenancy, all the basic costs of providing and managing the housing are paid out of the rent. It is true that there will sometimes be a service charge as well, but it normally covers things such as the provision of heating or communal lighting - things that, however necessary they may be, are peripheral to the central function of providing housing. As a result, service charges in rented property are usually quite moderate and cause little argument.

Contrast the position in leasehold housing. In both types of housing, the landlord is under a legal obligation to the residents to keep the property in good condition and to carry out any work necessary for that purpose; but the landlord of rented property is expected to meet the costs from the rent, whereas the freeholder of leasehold stock has no rent to fall back on (apart from the normally negligible ground rent). How, then, are major costs to be met when they arise? The answer, of course, is from the service charge, which is, therefore, of central importance to the management of leasehold property.

From the freeholder's point of view, the logic of service charges is impeccable. It is perfectly reasonable for freeholders to point out:

- that leaseholders benefit from the work because it has maintained or improved their homes; and
- that the fact that the work has been done means that leaseholders will get a better price when they come to sell; and
- that people that own their homes freehold have to find the money to meet costs of this kind.

To sum up the freeholder's position: the costs have been incurred; the work is for the benefit of the leaseholders; so the leaseholders must pay.

Leaseholders can point out in reply that someone that owns his home freehold can make his own choice when and how to do the repair; he can put up with a slightly leaking roof if he cannot afford to repair it. But freeholders of leasehold property have no such discretion: they are obliged under the lease to do their repairs promptly and if they did not would be liable to legal action by any leaseholder. So it is difficult for leaseholders to object to the principle of charges or to ask the freeholder to refrain from carrying out work or to delay it. In short, the purchase of a lease means the acceptance of a commitment to pay the appropriate share of costs. But does this mean that leaseholders have no scope to challenge or query service charges? No; under sections 18 to 30 of the Landlord and Tenant Act 1985, amended by the 1996 Housing Act and the 2002 Commonhold and Leasehold Reform Act they have extensive legal protection against improper or unreasonable charging by freeholders, and this is discussed later in the Chapter.

Unreasonable Service Charges
a: General Principles

Sections 18 to 30 of the Landlord and Tenant Act 1985, as amended by subsequent legislation, grant substantial protection to leaseholders of residential property. This protection was introduced after complaints of exploitation by unscrupulous leaseholders, who were alleged to be carrying out unnecessary, or even fictitious, repairs at extravagant prices, whilst not providing the information that would have enabled leaseholders to query the bill. The general effect of the Act is to require freeholders to provide leaseholders with full information about service charges and to consult them before expensive works are carried out. It must be stressed, however, that although the Act protects leaseholders against sharp practice by freeholders, and will prevent the recovery of **unreasonable** costs, it will support freeholders, provided they have gone through the necessary formalities described below, in the recovery of their **reasonable** costs, even if those costs are high. To take the example used above of the removal of asbestos from a block of flats: the fact that the average cost per flat is as high as £50,000 does not, in itself, make the charge unreasonable - to make use of the Act, objecting leaseholders have to show, when they are notified that the work is to be carried out (not when the bills arrive), that it was not necessary or could have been carried out cheaper.

A few leases, namely those granted under the right to buy by local authorities or registered housing associations, have some additional protection under the Housing Act 1985 (see below), but sections 18 to 30 apply to all residential leases where the service charge depends on how much the freeholder spends. They set out the key rules that freeholders must observe in order to recover the cost, including overheads, of 'services, repairs or improvements, maintenance or insurance', as well as the freeholder's costs of management. Sections 18 to 30 only apply to service charges, not to other charges such as ground rent.

It should be noted that failure by leaseholders to pay the service charge does not relieve the freeholder of the obligation to provide the services. The freeholder's remedy is to sue the leaseholder for the outstanding charges, or even to seek forfeiture of the lease (see below). Section 19 of the Act provides the key protection to leaseholders by laying down that service charges are recoverable only if they are 'reasonably incurred' and if the services or works are of a reasonable standard. This means that the charge:

-    must relate to some form of service, repair, maintenance, improvement, or insurance that the freeholder is required to provide under the lease;
-    must be reasonable (that is, the landlord may not recover costs incurred unnecessarily or extravagantly);
-    may cover overheads and management costs only if these too are reasonable.

In addition, the charge must normally be passed on to the leaseholders within 18 months of being incurred, and in some cases the freeholder must consult leaseholders before spending the money. These points are covered below.

The Housing Act 1996 gave leaseholders new powers to refer service charges to the Leasehold Valuation Tribunal (LVT). This is covered below (*Challenging Service Charges*).

b: Consultation with Leaseholders
Section 20 as amended by the 2002 Commonhold and Leasehold Reform Act provides extra protection where the cost of works is more than a certain limit. (£250 or more to the leaseholder). Costs above this level are irrecoverable unless the freeholder has taken steps to inform and consult tenants, although there are a exceptions in special cases (see below). If the leaseholders are not represented by a recognised tenants' association (for which see below) these steps are as follows:

Intention to carry out works: The landlord must write to all leaseholders stating the intention and reasons for carrying out work. There must be a notice period of 30 days.

Estimates At least two estimates must be obtained, of which at least   one must be from someone wholly unconnected from the freeholder (obviously a building firm that the freeholder owns or works for is not 'wholly unconnected'; nor is the freeholder's managing agent. Arguably, even a building firm with which the freeholder has no formal connexion could be 'connected' with him if he gives it so much work that it depends on him and is thus subject to his influence)

Notification to leaseholders The freeholder must either display a copy of the estimates somewhere they are likely to be seen by everyone liable to pay the service charges or preferably send copies to everyone liable to pay the charge

Consultation The notification must describe the works to be carried out and must seek comments and observations, giving a deadline for replies and an address in the UK to which they may be sent. The deadline must be at least a month after the notice was sent or displayed.

Freeholder's response The freeholder must 'have regard' to representations received. This does not mean, of course, that the freeholder must do what the leaseholders say. It does mean, however, that the freeholder must consider any comments received, and good freeholders often demonstrate that they have done so by sending a reasoned reply (i.e. not a form letter or bare acknowledgment, but a letter that responds specifically to any points made), even though the Act does not require them to.

It was mentioned above that there are special cases in which these requirements can be set aside. If a service charge is challenged, it is defence for the freeholder to show that the works were so urgent that there was no time for proper consultation. It is also possible for freeholders to enter into long term agreements to carry out works or provide services over a period of years; if so, they must consult before the agreement is entered into but they need not consult separately before each particular element of expenditure under the agreement. Finally, the Leasehold Valuation Tribunal has a general power to set aside the usual consultation requirements if it seems fair to do so.

Section 20 is important because it gives the leaseholders notification of any unusual items in the offing and gives them an opportunity to raise any concerns and objections. If the leaseholder has any reservations at all, it is vital that they be put before the freeholder at this stage. It is unlikely, in the event of legal action later, that courts or LVTs will support a leaseholder that raised no objection until the bill arrived.

It is surprisingly common for freeholders and their agents to fail to comply with the requirements of section 20. This comment applies not only where the freehold is owned by an individual or a relatively small organisation (where mistakes might be more understandable) but also where the freeholder is a large, well resourced body like a local authority (which should be well able to understand and carry out its legal duties).

As a result leaseholders are often paying service charges that are not due, so all leaseholders should, before paying a service charge containing unusual items, ensure that section 20, if it applies, has been scrupulously followed. If not, they can refuse to pay.

c: Other Protection for Leaseholders

Grant-aided works: If the freeholder has received a grant towards the cost of carrying out the works, the amount must be deducted from the service charge levied on leaseholders.

Late charging: Service charge bills may not normally include costs incurred more than eighteen months earlier. The freeholder may, however, notify leaseholders within the eighteen month period that they will have to pay a certain cost, and then bill them later. This may happen if, for instance, the freeholder is in dispute with a contractor about the level of a bill or the standard of work.

Pre-charging: Sometimes a lease will contain a provision allowing the freeholder to make a charge to cover future costs besides those already incurred. This practice, which is perfectly lawful in itself, may be in the interests of the leaseholders by spreading over a longer period the cost of major works. It is, however, subject to the same overall requirement of reasonableness.

Court costs: Section 20C provides protection against a specific abuse of the service charge system by freeholders. Previously, freeholders tended to regard their legal costs as part of the process of managing the housing and thus as recoverable from leaseholders. Such an attitude is not necessarily unreasonable: if, for instance, the freeholder is suing a builder for poor work, he is, in effect, acting on behalf of all the leaseholders and it is fair that they should pay any legal costs. But suppose the freeholder were involved in legal proceedings against one of the leaseholders: if the leaseholder lost, he would probably to be ordered to pay the freeholder's costs as well as his own; but if the freeholder lost, and had to pay both his own and the leaseholder's costs, he could simply, under the previous law, recover the money as part of the management element in the service charge. This meant that the freeholder was able to pursue legal action against leaseholders without fear of heavy legal costs in the event of defeat, the very factor that deters most people from too ready a resort to law. To prevent this, section 20C allows leaseholders to seek an order that the freeholder's legal costs must not be counted towards service charges.

Service charges held on trust: Section 42 of the Landlord and Tenant Act 1987 further strengthened the position of leaseholders by laying down that the freeholder, or the freeholder's agent, must hold service charge monies in a suitable interest-bearing trust fund that will ensure that the money is protected and cannot be seized by the freeholder's creditors if the freeholder goes bankrupt or into liquidation. However, public sector freeholders, notably local authorities and registered housing associations, are exempt from this requirement.

Administration charges: These are the freeholder's costs incurred in complying with leaseholders' requests for information and approvals under the terms of the lease. All such charges must be reasonable. Any demand for administration charges must be accompanied by a summary of leaseholders' rights and obligations in relation to them. The LVT has the power to decide whether or not an administration charge is payable, and if so, to whom and by whom together with the amount, date payable and the manner in which it is paid.

Ground rent: Strictly, this is not part of the service charge but as it is usually collected along with it, it is covered here. It will be specified in the lease and is usually a fairly modest annual sum in the order of £50 or £100. Leaseholders should note that, unlike the service charge and most other charges, the ground rent is not intended to compensate the freeholder for any costs or trouble; it is simply a payment by which the leaseholder recognises that ultimately the property belongs to the freeholder. Therefore freeholders are under no obligation to demonstrate that it is reasonable. But it is not payable unless the landlord has issued a formal request for it, which must specify the amount of the payment, the date on which the leaseholder is liable to pay it and the date (if different) on which it would have been payable under the lease. The date for payment must be at least 30 days and not more than 60 days after the date of the notice.

Insurance: Usually, any insurance required under the lease will be taken out by the freeholder and this is discussed below. Occasionally, however, the leaseholder will be required to take out insurance with a company nominated by the freeholder. If the leaseholder thinks he is getting a poor deal, he can apply to the county court or a Leasehold Valuation Tribunal which, if satisfied that the insurance is unsatisfactory or the premiums are unreasonably high, can order the freeholder to nominate another insurer.

'Period of Grace': When a dwelling is sold under the right to buy by a local authority or non-charitable housing association, the purchaser is given an estimate of service charges for the following five years. This estimate is the maximum recoverable during that time. Some purchasers under the right to buy have, however, had a very rude shock when the five year period of grace expires - see *Exceptionally High Service Charges* below.

117

d: The role of a recognised tenants' association

The tenants who are liable to pay for the provision of services may, if they wish, form a recognised tenants' association (RTA) under section 29 of the Landlord and Tenant Act 1985. Note that leaseholders count as tenants for this purpose (see Chapter One, where it explained that legally the two terms are interchangeable). If the freeholder refuses to give a notice recognising the RTA, it may apply for recognition to any member of the local Rent Assessment Committee panel ('Rent Assessment Committee' is the official term for a Leasehold Valuation Tribunal when it is carrying out certain functions, not otherwise relevant to leaseholders, under the Rent Act 1977).

An important benefit of having a RTA is that it has the right, at the beginning of the consultation process, to recommend persons or organisations that should be invited to submit estimates. However, the freeholder is under no obligation to accept these recommendations.

Another advantage is that the RTA can, whether the freeholder likes it or not, appoint a qualified surveyor to advise on matters relating to service charges. The surveyor has extensive rights to inspect the freeholder's documentation and take copies, and can enforce these rights in court if necessary.

Against these benefits must be set the principal disadvantage of having a RTA, namely that it weakens the freeholder's obligation to consult individual leaseholders. Where there is a RTA, the freeholder, instead of having to supply copies of the estimates to all leaseholders (or place copies where they are likely to be seen), merely has to send them to the secretary of the RTA, and the individual leaseholders must make do with summaries.

Leaseholders - and for that matter, ordinary periodic tenants - should therefore weigh carefully the advantages and disadvantages of setting up a RTA. If they decide against, there is nothing to prevent them from forming an **unrecognised** tenants' (or leaseholders') association, which can represent their interests to the freeholder, provided that it is made clear that formal recognition under section 29 is not being sought.

Challenging Service Charges

The Landlord and Tenant Act not only allows leaseholders to take action against unreasonable behaviour by the freeholder; it also enables them to take the initiative. This is done in two ways: by giving leaseholders rights to demand information, and by allowing them to challenge the reasonableness of the charge.

Any demand for service charges must include details about leaseholders' rights and how they can challenge the charges. If this is not done the leaseholder may withhold payment without penalty.

a: Right to information

Freeholders must provide a written summary of costs counting towards the service charge. It must be sent to the leaseholder within six months of the end of the period it covers. The service charge need not be paid until the summary is provided.

The law lays down some minimum requirements for the summary. It must:

- cover all the costs incurred during the twelve months it covers, even if they were included in service charge bills of an earlier or later period (see above for late charging and pre-charging);
- show how the costs incurred by the freeholder are reflected in the service charges paid, or to be paid, by leaseholders;
- say whether it includes any work covered by a grant (see above);
- distinguish: (a) those costs incurred for which the freeholder was not billed during the period; (b) those for which he was billed and did not pay; (c) those for which he paid bills.

If it covers five or more dwellings, the summary must, in addition, be certified by a qualified accountant as being a fair summary, complying with the Act, and supported by appropriate documentation.

The purpose of these rules is to put leaseholders in a position to challenge their service charges. After receiving the summary, the leaseholder has six months in which to ask the freeholder to make facilities available so that he can inspect the documents supporting the summary (bills, receipts, and so on) and take copies or extracts. The freeholder must make the facilities available within 21 days after such a request; the inspection itself must be free, although the freeholder can make a reasonable charge for the copies and extracts. Failure to provide these facilities, like failure to supply the summary, is punishable by a fine of up to £2500.

Very similar rules apply where the lease allows, or requires, the freeholder to take out insurance against certain contingencies, such as major repair, and to recover the premiums through the service charge. This is not unreasonable in itself and will, indeed, often be in the interests of leaseholders. The danger is, however, that the freeholder, knowing that the premiums are, in effect, being paid by someone else, has no incentive to shop around for the best deal. Section 30A of the Landlord and Tenant Act 1985 therefore lays down that leaseholders, or the secretary of the recognised tenants' association if there is one, may ask the freeholder for information about the policy. Failure to supply it, or to make facilities to inspect relevant documents available if requested to do so, is an offence incurring a fine of up to £2500.

It must be acknowledged that the rules allowing leaseholders to require information about service charges are, particularly in view of the £2500 fines, fairly onerous from the freeholder's point of view. It is the purpose of this book to inform leaseholders of their rights, not to make life difficult for freeholders: nevertheless, it must be admitted that if leaseholders wish to pursue a policy of confronting freeholders, and to cause them as much trouble as possible, sections 21, 22, and 30A offer plenty of scope.

b: Challenging a service charge

Any leaseholder liable to pay a service charge, and for that matter any freeholder levying one, may refer the charge to a Leasehold Valuation Tribunal to determine its reasonableness. This may be done at any time, even when the service in question is merely a proposal by the freeholder (for instance, for future major works). But the LVT will not consider a service charge if:

- it has already been approved by a court; or

-       if the leaseholder has agreed to refer it to arbitration; or
-       if the leaseholder has agreed it.

The first of these exceptions is obvious and the second is unlikely to apply very often. The third one is the problem: leaseholders should be careful, in their dealings with freeholders, to say or do nothing that could be taken to imply that they agree with any service charge that is in any way doubtful.

The LVT will consider:

-       whether a service charge is payable and if so when, how, and by whom;
-       whether the freeholder's costs of services, repairs, maintenance, insurance, or management are reasonably incurred;
-       whether the services or works are of a reasonable standard; and
-       whether any payment required in advance is reasonable.

The fees for application to a LVT can be obtained from the LVT and will usually change annually. Appeal against a LVT decision is not to the courts but to the Lands Tribunal.

By section 19 of the Landlord and Tenant Act 1985, any service charge deemed unreasonable by the LVT is irrecoverable by the freeholder. The determination of service charges by the LVT also plays an important part in the rules governing the use of forfeiture to recover service charges. It is to this that we now turn.

Forfeiture for Unpaid Service Charges
Forfeiture was mentioned at the end of Chapter Two. Briefly, it is the right of the freeholder to resume possession of the property if the leaseholder breaches the lease.

By section 81 of the Housing Act 1996, as amended by the 2002 Leasehold and Commonhold Reform Act, forfeiture for an unpaid service charge is available to the freeholder only if:

- the leaseholder has agreed the charge; or
- the charge has been upheld through post-dispute arbitration or by the Leasehold Valuation Tribunal or a court.

Regarding the first of these, it is necessary only to reiterate the warning to leaseholders to say or do nothing that could possibly be construed as representing their agreement to any service charge about whose legitimacy they have the slightest doubt.

Regarding the second, it should be noted that where the leaseholder has not agreed the service charge, proceedings before the LVT or a court or post-dispute arbitration are necessary before the freeholder can forfeit the lease.

A further requirement is that the amount of money involved must either exceed a certain amount or have been outstanding for a minimum period of time. The Government will set these limits by order. It is currently proposed that the minimum amount will be £350 and the minimum period three years, but this is yet to be confirmed. Note that it is necessary for only one of the requirements to be satisfied.

To sum up, before the freeholder can forfeit:
- it must have been formally decided that the service charge is due,
- the amount must exceed the minimum amount or have been owed for the minimum time, and
- a section 146 notice must have been served (but this requirement does not apply if the service charge is reserved as rent).

The freeholder can still begin the process by issuing a section 146 notice but it must state that the forfeiture cannot proceed until the requirements of section 81 have been met.

It remains to be seen how these new provisions will operate in practice. Their purpose is to prevent freeholders from using the draconian threat of forfeiture to pressurise leaseholders into paying disputed service charges, and to this extent the position of leaseholders has been greatly strengthened. The danger is that freeholders may respond by getting disputed charges before the LVT as quickly as possible so that forfeiture becomes available if the charges are upheld. Another concern is that some leaseholders, faced with service charges they are unwilling to pay but about which there is no dispute, may be unable to resist the temptation to invent spurious grounds for objection in order to deprive the freeholder of the weapon of forfeiture; this tactic is likely to provoke even relatively easy-going freeholders into legal action.

Once the leaseholder has agreed the service charge or it has been upheld by the LVT or a court or through arbitration, forfeiture becomes a serious threat and in this situation the advice can only be to pay the charge if at all possible. If, however, the leaseholder is unable to pay he may find it helpful to contact his mortgagee (if any). For the mortgagee, forfeiture is a disaster because it is likely to be left with a large unsecured debt on its hands, so many mortgagees in this situation will pay the service charges and add the cost to the outstanding mortgage. This does not solve the leaseholder's long term problem - that his lease commits him to payments he is unable to meet - but it will give him a little breathing space and may enable him to sell up and pay off his debts.

Some leaseholders, especially those of longer standing, may be living on fixed incomes and have very little cash to spare, even though their property is quite valuable. Sometimes their mortgage has been paid off altogether; even if it is still outstanding, it will probably be very small in relation to the value of the property. Leaseholders that find themselves in this 'property-rich, cash-poor' situation may find it helpful to look at equity release schemes, operated by a number of financial institutions.

14

ENFRANCHISEMENT AND EXTENSION OF LEASES

What Are Enfranchisement and Extension?

Chapter One set out the legal theory underlying the relationship between freeholder and leaseholder, and explained that a lease must be limited in time and that, in principle, at the end of that time the lease finishes and the property reverts to the freeholder.

It has always been, and still is, open to the freeholder and the leaseholder to negotiate some different arrangement. For instance, they might agree that the freeholder will buy the unexpired term of the lease from the leaseholder: but, because the freeholder and the leaseholder cannot be the same person, this will have the effect of extinguishing the lease and the leave the freeholder on sole possession of the land as if the lease had never existed. Alternatively, the freeholder might agree to sell the freehold to the leaseholder: again, and for the same reason, this will extinguish the lease, but this time it is the former leaseholder that will be left in sole freehold possession. The sale of the freehold to the leaseholder is called 'enfranchisement' of the lease, because it is freed, or 'enfranchised', from the overriding freehold, and replaces it. A further possibility is that the freeholder and leaseholder may agree to extend the lease beyond its original term. If agreements of this kind are negotiated, it is entirely for the freeholder and leaseholder to settle the conditions and the price.

In recent years, however, the law has forced freeholders, in certain circumstances, to sell freeholds or extend leases, whether they wish to or not. This has been done by three pieces of legislation: the Leasehold Reform Act 1967, the Landlord and Tenant Act 1987, and the Leasehold Reform, Housing and Urban Development Act 1993 (although all three Acts have been amended

124

by later legislation, particularly the Housing Act 1996 and the Commonhold and Leasehold Reform Act 2002). The Housing and Regeneration Act 2008 also makes amendments to the 1967 Leasehold Reform Act, which have not yet come into effect. The Acts are dealt with in the order they were passed, which means that the most important right - that of leaseholders of flats - is left to last. This is fitting, because, as is explained below, it was a Parliamentary afterthought; the Government originally had no intention of granting such an important right.

But before looking at the legislation, it is important to establish why extension and enfranchisement are important to the average leaseholder.

Extension of a Lease Some enlightened freeholders automatically extend the lease whenever it is assigned, so that if a lease that was originally granted for 125 years is assigned after 30, the assignee gets a lease not for 95 years, as one might expect, but for 125. From the leaseholder's point of view, such an arrangement is extremely valuable because otherwise the lease represents a wasting asset, whose value will drop sharply as the end of the term approaches. The arrangement can also benefit the freeholder by making the lease more valuable at the time of its original sale. But most leases are unaffected by assignment and would expire on the originally determined date were it not for legislation that obliges freeholders, in certain circumstances, to grant a fresh 90 year lease to the leaseholder: this is described below.

Individual Enfranchisement of a lease Legislation, described below, now allows the leaseholder to acquire the freehold, in certain circumstances, whether or not the freeholder agrees. If not for this, the leaseholder would find that his home had reverted to the ownership of the freeholder at the end the lease and he would have to buy it back (assuming the freeholder were willing to sell). The freeholder is, however, entitled to compensation.

Collective Enfranchisement of Leases The problem with leasehold enfranchisement is that the property concerned must be capable of being held on a freehold basis. Where it stands on a distinct and definable piece of land this does not present a problem: the freehold of the land is transferred to the leaseholder and, as explained in Chapter One, any buildings on it are automatically transferred too. But if the property is only part of a larger building, it may not be attached to its own unique piece of land in the same way, so individual enfranchisement is not available to flat owners. If they wish to enfranchise, therefore, they have to agree among themselves that a single person or body will buy the freehold on behalf of all of them, while they continue to hold leases of their individual flats.

This is called 'collective enfranchisement', although this term is misleading because technically the leases have not been enfranchised at all: all that has happened is a change from the original freeholder to a new one nominated by the leaseholders. Since the passage of the Commonhold and Leasehold Reform Act 2002, this new freeholder has to be a special type of organisation called a 'Right to Enfranchise' (or 'RtE') company.

Rights to Enfranchise and Extend Leases: General Principles
The remainder of this Chapter sets out what rights leaseholders have if they wish to extend or enfranchise their leases. It is stressed at the outset, however, that anyone contemplating such a step should obtain independent legal advice from a solicitor, and in most cases also from a valuer. This applies not only if the lease is being enfranchised or extended under one of the Acts, but also if it is being done voluntarily by agreement with the freeholder. The issues involved are potentially very complex and attempting to deal with them without expert advice could put your home at risk.

The Acts are available to what they describe as 'qualifying tenants': but the exact meaning of the term varies depending which right is being exercised under which Act. Usually, but not always, the term is defined in a way that excludes ordinary tenants and confines it to leaseholders. The key issue is the existence of a long lease (see below). Other former tests, relating to residence or the amount of rent, were abolished by the 2002 Act.

A Long Lease For most purposes under the Acts, the leaseholder must own a lease originally granted for at least 21 years. Note that this is the term when the lease was granted, not the period it still has to run, so that a 99 year lease granted in 1910 is still a long lease in 2003 even though it has only six years to go. Recent legislation has put an end to a number of devices formerly inserted into leases by freeholders in order to avoid having to extend or enfranchise leases.

Some were bizarre: leases were made terminable on extraneous events, such as royal marriages or deaths, because the lease was not regarded as long if it depended on an event that could occur at any time. These evasions have been of no effect since the 1993 Act, which provides that leases containing them shall be treated as long leases.

Exemptions There are various exemptions from the Acts.
- If the freeholder is a charitable housing trust and the dwelling is provided as part of its charitable work, the leaseholder can neither extend nor enfranchise the lease (unless the charity agrees).
- The Acts do not apply to business leases. This applies even if a dwelling is included: for instance, if the lease of a shop includes the flat above it.
- The Acts do not apply if the property is within the precincts of a cathedral or owned by the Crown (however, it is possible that the Crown authorities will agree to a voluntary extension or enfranchisement of the lease). Some properties owned by the National Trust are also exempt.
- Other exemptions apply not across the board but to particular types of transaction. These are covered as the various Acts are discussed below.

Leasehold Reform Act 1967: Leases of Houses
The first legislation to deal with leasehold extension and enfranchisement was the Leasehold Reform Act 1967. This Act is still in force, but is not relevant to most residential leaseholders, who will get more benefit from later legislation. It can therefore be dealt with fairly briefly. The Act relates only to residential leases of

houses - not flats. With certain exceptions, a leaseholder qualifies to use it if he has held for at least two years a lease originally granted for 21 years or more. The Act allows qualifying leaseholders to acquire the freehold of their homes, or, if they prefer, extend the lease for 50 years.

The usual exemptions (see above) apply to the 1967 Act. In addition, it does not apply to most shared ownership leases granted by housing associations.

Most leaseholders qualifying to make use of the 1967 Act have long since done so, because the benefits of owning the freehold outweigh the drawback of having to pay the freeholder the difference (usually not very great) between the freehold and leasehold value of the house.

Generally speaking, therefore, remaining leasehold houses will be those to which the Act does not apply, either because the freeholder is exempt or because the house is attached to other property. The last point is an important limitation on the 1967 Act: if the land on which the house stands is shared by any other property not covered by the lease, however small it may be compared with the house, the Act cannot be used. It may, however, be possible for the leaseholder of such a house to use the new rights in the Leasehold Reform, Housing and Urban Development Act 1993.

The procedure for enfranchisement under the 1967 Act is as follows.

- The leaseholder serves a notice on the freeholder stating that he wishes to claim the freehold (or extend the lease). This notice should give particulars of the property and the lease.

- Within two months, the freeholder must send a counter notice that either accepts the leaseholder's claim or gives reasons for rejecting it. The freeholder may ask the leaseholder for a deposit of £25 or thrice the annual ground rent, whichever is more, and for proof that he holds the lease and meets the residence test. The leaseholder has 14 days to produce the money and 21 days to produce the proof.

- If the freeholder does not submit a counter notice within two months, the leaseholder's claim is automatically accepted. If the freeholder's counter notice unfairly rejects the leaseholder's claim, the leaseholder may apply to the county court.

Obviously, the freeholder is justified in rejecting the claim if the property does not come under the Act or if the leaseholder does not qualify. In addition, the freeholder may reject the claim if he acquired the house before 18th February 1966 and needs the house, on expiry of the lease, as a home for himself or a member of his family. He may also refuse to extend the lease (but not to enfranchise it) if he plans to redevelop the property.

Once it has been established that the leaseholder may enfranchise, a price must be agreed; if this is not possible, it will be set by a leasehold valuation tribunal. The Act lays down that the price should be the value of the freehold if it were being sold willingly but on the assumption that the lease were continuing and would be renewable under the Act. In effect, this formula means that the leaseholder is obliged to pay for what he is acquiring (the freehold) but not for what he has already got (the lease). Once a price has been agreed, or set by tribunal, either the freeholder or the leaseholder has one month to serve a notice on the other requiring him to complete. The freeholder must convey the freehold as a fee simple absolute, or (as a non-lawyer would say) outright.

Landlord and Tenant Act 1987: First Refusal and Mismanagement
The Landlord and Tenant Act 1987 was chiefly concerned with enabling leaseholders to protect themselves against unreasonable service charges, and it made numerous amendments to tighten the rules originally laid down in the Landlord and Tenant Act 1985 (see Chapter Three).

In addition, it granted leaseholders the important right of first refusal if the freehold of their property is sold. It also allowed leaseholders to acquire the freehold if the property is being mismanaged: however, this right is little used because of the difficult procedures involved, and although it remains on the statute book it is likely to fall into complete disuse because the 1993 Act has now given leaseholders the same right without having to prove mismanagement.

a: First refusal

The right of first refusal was granted in order to stop the practice of selling freeholds, without any reference to the leaseholders or other occupiers, from one person or organisation to another so that leaseholders were often completely in the dark about who the ultimate freeholder was (when this sort of thing went on the eventual freeholder often turned out to be a company existing on paper only and based somewhere completely inaccessible like the Cayman Islands - see Chapter Two for legislation passed at the same time forcing freeholders to give their name and an address in the UK for the service of legal notices). The right of first refusal remains important because it is sometimes available when ordinary collective enfranchisement, under the 1993 Act, is not possible.

The 1987 Act says that if the freeholder intends to sell the freehold he must first offer it to the leaseholders and other qualifying tenants. There are, however, some exceptions: the Act does not apply if the freeholder is selling to a member of his family, or if he lives in the block himself; nor does it apply if the block is not chiefly residential. In addition, virtually all public sector freeholders are excluded from the Act: this means local authorities, registered housing associations, and various other bodies. It is, however, unlikely that this sort of body will wish to sell its freehold. But if none of these exceptions applies, and if the majority of qualifying tenants (including leaseholders) wish to buy, they must be given the opportunity to meet the freeholder's price. For the purpose of defining a 'majority' there can be only one qualifying tenant in respect of each flat: in other words, joint tenants (or joint leaseholders) have only one 'vote' between them, and must agree between themselves how it will be used.

'Qualifying tenants' are:

- tenants entitled to a Fair Rent under the 1977 Rent Act: that is, most tenants of self-contained dwellings holding a tenancy originally granted on or before 14th January 1989, but excluding council tenants; and

* leaseholders, except for business leaseholders (the normal 21 year minimum does not apply).

If the qualifying tenants and freeholder cannot agree terms for the sale, the freeholder is able to sell to someone else. However, the qualifying tenants must be informed of this sale and, most importantly, of the price. They then have the right to buy the freehold from the new owner at whatever price he paid. This is designed to stop the original freeholder from asking the qualifying tenants for an excessive price that they are bound to reject, then selling to someone else at a lower price. Similarly, if the freeholder carries out a sale without informing the qualifying tenants, they have the right to buy from the new freeholder for the same price that he paid. Procedure under the 1987 for the right of first refusal is as follows.

* The freeholder notifies all qualifying tenants of his desire to sell and of the price at which he is willing to do so (including any non-monetary element). The notice must state the proposed method of sale: for instance, by conveyance or by auction.

* The freeholder must give the qualifying tenants at least two months to respond; and, if they say they wish to buy, at least a further two months (28 days if the sale is to be by auction) to come up with a nominee purchaser to acquire the freehold on their behalf. This could conceivably be in an individual or an organisation that already exists, but is much likelier to be a company set up specially for the purpose by the qualifying tenants, and under their control.

* During this period, the landlord and the qualifying tenants may wish to take the opportunity to negotiate the price.

* If a majority of the qualifying tenants have put forward a nominee purchaser and agreed with the freeholder on a price, the freeholder may not sell to anyone else.

*   If the qualifying tenants fail to put forward a nominee purchaser, or if a mutually acceptable price is not agreed, the freeholder has twelve months to sell to someone else in accordance with the original notice (by auction, if that was the method specified; and in any other case for a price not less than that originally offered to the qualifying tenants). If no sale has taken place within twelve months, the freeholder must start the procedure again from scratch if he wishes to sell.

b: Mismanagement: the right to enfranchise

As mentioned above, the 1987 Act is designed mainly to protect leaseholders against mismanagement and sharp practice by freeholders. It therefore gives them the power of collective enfranchisement against a freeholder guilty of serious or repeated breach of his obligations. The power is available to long leaseholders, but a leaseholder does not qualify to use this part of the Act if he owns long leases of three or more flats in the block.

Moreover, this part of the 1987 Act does not apply where the freeholder is the Crown or a public body such as a local authority or a registered housing association. Nor does it apply when the freeholder resides in the property himself. It is available only where two-thirds or more of the flats in the block are let on long leases, and in blocks of ten flats or fewer a higher proportion is required. The court can make an order transferring the freehold to the leaseholders' nominee only if a manager appointed (see Chapter Two) by a court or LVT has controlled the premises for at least two years, unless the leaseholders can show both

-     that the freeholder is and is likely to remain in breach of his obligations under the lease; and

-     that the mere appointment of a manager would be an inadequate remedy.

All these restrictions suggest that the Act envisages that enfranchisement on grounds of mismanagement is very much a last resort; indeed, it is necessary for the leaseholders to take their case to court and get permission before they can proceed. The right was seldom used and, although it remains available in theory, in practice it has been superseded by the 1993 Act, which gives most leaseholders the right of collective enfranchisement whatever the standard of management and with no need for a court order. Nevertheless, it is just possible there is a body of leaseholders somewhere willing to use the 1987 Act rather than the 1993 Act. The procedures for collective enfranchisement following mismanagement are therefore briefly set out here, with a warning that the general recommendation to employ a solicitor applies with special emphasis if this route is chosen.

- At least two-thirds of the qualifying leaseholders must serve a preliminary notice informing the freeholder that they intend to go to court to acquire the freehold. The notice must give the names and addresses of the leaseholder and the grounds for their application; the freeholder should also be given a reasonable deadline to rectify the problems if it is possible for him to do so.

- The leaseholders must apply to the court, giving their reasons for dissatisfaction and requesting an order to transfer the freehold to their nominee purchaser (probably, as with other forms of collective enfranchisement, a company set up for the purpose).

- If satisfied that it is fair to do so, the court will transfer the block to the nominee purchaser. The price will have to be agreed by the leaseholders and the freeholder; or, if (as is likely) this is not possible, by a Leasehold Valuation Tribunal. The price will be the value of the freehold on the assumption that all the leases are to continue: there will be no additional 'marriage value' (see below), and this is one of the few reasons for preferring to use the 1987 Act rather than the 1993 Act.

Leasehold Reform, Housing and Urban Development Act 1993: Collective Enfranchisement and Lease Extension

The 1993 Act greatly extended the rights of leaseholders: its passage through Parliament was, indeed, strongly contested by large private freeholders, who claimed that it was unfair to them as property owners. It made a number of adjustments, dealt with above, to existing rights under the 1967 and 1987 Acts; in addition, it created two new rights for leaseholders of flats. These are the right to collective enfranchisement, and the right to extend individual leases.

a: Collective enfranchisement under the 1993 Act

In outline, the right to collective enfranchisement under the 1993 Act is similar to, but much easier than, collective enfranchisement under the 1987 Act. Under both schemes, qualifying leaseholders choose a purchaser to whom the freeholder can be forced to sell; but under the 1993 Act there is no need for a court order and no need to show that there has been mismanagement.

The 1993 Act is available to long leaseholders, provided that at least two-thirds of the flats are let on long leases and at least half the eligible leaseholders are involved.

However, the block may not be enfranchised if it falls within the normal exemptions, or if it is not chiefly residential, or if it is a house converted into four flats or fewer with a resident freeholder who owned the freehold before the conversion. Even if there is a resident freeholder, however, the scheme applies to houses converted into five flats or more and to purpose-built blocks even if they contain only two flats.

There are special provisions for any parts of the building that are occupied by people or organisations other than qualifying leaseholders. Some flats may be let to periodic tenants, for instance, and a block that faces a main road may well contain shop units on the ground floor. Any such parts may, and in some cases must, be leased back to the original freeholder when the block is acquired. 'Leaseback', as it is called, is mandatory for any flats let to periodic tenants (secure or assured) by a local authority or a registered housing association. This means that they can continue as council (or association) tenants, and do not lose any legal rights. It is up to the freeholder (not the leaseholders) whether he wants a leaseback of other flats or premises, such as business units or flats occupied by non-qualifying leaseholders. Unless the parties agree otherwise, leaseback is for 999 years at a notional rent - in other words, on terms typical of residential leases, and discussed in Chapters One and Two. The leaseholders must choose a purchaser. Formerly, this could be any individual or organisation that had the confidence of the others and was willing to undertake the role. The 2002 Act has, however, tightened the rules by providing that only a 'Right to Enfranchise' ('RtE') company can take over the freehold. This protects leaseholders' rights by ensuring that the enfranchisee is a body in which they all have a right to be involved, but the Government has taken powers to lay down what the constitution of the RtE company must be, and it is likely that many leaseholders will find the prescribed constitution unwieldy and inflexible.

Setting up and running the RtE company is only one of the responsibilities in which collective enfranchisement will involve leaseholders. They will also have to pay both their own and the freeholder's legal and professional costs. And above all, they must pay the purchase price of the freehold, which, unless they come to an agreement with the freeholder, will be decided by a leasehold valuation tribunal in accordance with rules laid down in the Act. These say that the price consists of two components: the open market value and the 'marriage value'.

According to the formula in the Act, the **open market value** should reflect the income the freeholder would have received from rents plus the prospect of regaining possession of the parts of the building currently let. How much this is will depend on how the building is being used now. If, as will often be the case, it consists wholly of flats let on long leases with many years to run, the open market value will probably be low because ground rents are usually very modest and the prospect of regaining possession is a distant one and of correspondingly little value. But if the building contains lucrative business or periodic tenancies, perhaps quite short term, and if the freeholder elects not to have these leased back, the open market value will be substantial.

The other component in the price, the **'marriage value'**, is based on the assumption that, combined (as they will be after enfranchisement), the leases and the freehold have a greater value than they would if sold separately. The Act says the freeholder is entitled to half this amount. In most cases, however, especially where the leases have a long time to run, the marriage value will be low, and where a lease has more than 80 years to run the marriage value will be disregarded. Altogether the costs of enfranchisement may be considerable. It is therefore prudent for leaseholders to explore the ground before committing themselves. This can be done by any qualifying leaseholder by serving a notice on the freeholder (or whomever the leaseholder pays rent to) under section 11 of the Act. Such a notice obliges the freeholder to disclose, within 28 days, information that will be relevant to any sale, such as title deeds, surveyor's reports, planning restrictions, and so on. This will allow the leaseholders to take an informed view of whether they wish to go for collective enfranchisement and, if so, on what terms. At this stage, they should take their time and think it over carefully, for if they proceed further they will be obliged to pay the freeholder's legal costs if they later decide to withdraw.

It may be appropriate, too, at this stage, for the leaseholders to ask the freeholder whether he is prepared to consider a voluntary sale without forcing all concerned to go through the somewhat elaborate procedures laid down by the 1993 Act. A reasonable freeholder, since he will be aware that he can be forced to sell anyway, may well be willing to discuss this.

If the leaseholders decide to go ahead with collective enfranchisement under the 1993 Act, they must form a 'Right to Enfranchise' ('RtE') company. The purpose of the company is to act as the vehicle for the enfranchisement and subsequently to own the freehold of the block.

Every RtE company has to operate in accordance with a constitution (the 'memorandum and articles') laid down by Government. The aim is to ensure that all leaseholders have a fair chance to take part, but it is likely that many leaseholders will find that the constitution laid down for them is extremely bureaucratic and unwieldy, especially when it is remembered that many enfranchisements will be carried out in small blocks where they may be only a dozen leaseholders or even fewer.

All qualifying leaseholders are entitled to be members of the RtE company, but in practice it is controlled by 'participating members', namely those leaseholders that have served on the company a 'participation notice'. When the company is set up all qualifying leaseholders must be sent a formal notice inviting them to participate by serving such a notice. Once the enfranchisement takes place, membership of the RtE company is confined to participating members.

The RtE company serves an initial notice (also called a 'section 13 notice') giving the names and addresses of the leaseholders involved and exactly specifying what property they wish to enfranchise and which parts, if any, they will lease back. The notice must also propose a price, and give the freeholder at least two months to reply. Once the initial notice has been served, the freeholder may not sell the freehold to any third party.

From now on, the RtE company handles proceedings on behalf of the leaseholders. The freeholder may require the RtE company to provide evidence to show that the participating leaseholders are qualified under the Act. If the RtE company does not respond within 21 days, the freeholder may in some circumstances treat the initial notice as being withdrawn.

By the date specified in the initial notice, the freeholder must serve a counter notice either accepting the leaseholders' right to enfranchise or giving reasons for rejecting it. The freeholder must also state whether he accepts the details of the leaseholders' proposal as regards price and exactly what is to be included in the sale, and must say whether he wishes to lease back any parts of the property (in addition to those where leaseback is mandatory). The freeholder may refuse to exercise his right to lease back parts of the premises let on lucrative business lets because the effect of this will be to increase the price and, perhaps, deter the leaseholders from continuing. In the unlikely event that most of the leaseholders' leases have less than five years to run, the freeholder has the right to stop the enfranchisement if he can satisfy a court that he intends to redevelop the block.

The intention of the Act is that after the freeholder's counter notice the parties will attempt to resolve any differences, so that the sale of the freehold can proceed on agreed terms. Often, however, agreement will be impossible and in that case the matters in dispute are referred to a leasehold valuation tribunal. Such a referral must take place at least two months, and not more than six months, after the freeholder's counter notice; if no agreement is reached, and no referral made, after six months, the initial notice will be deemed withdrawn.

Once the terms have been settled, the parties have two months to exchange contracts. At the end of this time, the nominee purchaser has a further two months to ask a court to transfer the freehold on the terms agreed (or determined by the tribunal); or the freeholder may ask the court to rule that the initial notice shall be treated as being withdrawn.

To sum up, the procedure is complex and demanding, which is why it has been little used even though several years have passed since it became available under the 1993 Act. The 2002 Act has made the process more favourable to leaseholders in some ways, but these improvements are more than offset by the further layer of difficulty added by the new requirement to set up a RtE company. All in all, it seems likely that these procedures will not be much used, but their existence may be helpful in persuading freeholders to negotiate seriously if leaseholders want to buy the freehold.

b: Lease extension under the 1993 Act

Although the right to collective enfranchisement, as created by the 1993 Act, is of great importance because it makes a fundamental shift in the relationship between freeholders and leaseholders, the complex procedures mean that it is likely to be relatively seldom used. On the other hand, the right to a new lease, which was also created (for flat owners) by the 1993 Act, is likely to prove of immense practical benefit to thousands of leaseholders, not least because it can be exercised on an individual basis. It is ironic that this, the most valuable right leaseholders derive from the 1993 Act, was something of a Parliamentary afterthought. The original intention was to create the right to collective enfranchisement, with individual lease extensions as very much a second best option available only to leaseholders that for some reason were disqualified from collective enfranchisement. But as the legislation made its way through Parliament the right to extend leases was granted to more and more categories of leaseholder, and by the time the Act became law it had become a general right.

The principle is similar to the right to lease extension that house owners enjoy under the 1967 Act. Anyone that has owned for at least two years a long lease of a flat qualifies to extend it under the 1993 Act. The former low rent test and residence test were abolished by the 2002 Act. The freeholder is required to grant a new lease running for the remainder of the term of the old lease plus an additional 90 years, so that if the old lease had 40 years to go the new one will be granted for 130. In other respects, however, the terms of the new lease will be the same as, or very similar to, the old one.

The leaseholder will have to pay the freeholder a sum consisting of two components calculated in accordance with rules set out in the Act. The first represents the reduction in the market value of the freehold that results because the freeholder will now have to wait to regain possession for 90 years longer than would otherwise have been the case. The less time the old lease had to run, the higher this component is likely to be. The second component is the 'marriage value', reflecting the higher value of a longer lease. As with collective enfranchisement, the freeholder is entitled to 50% of the marriage value, but it is disregarded altogether if the old lease has more than 80 years to go.

A leaseholder who is contemplating a lease extension should begin by serving a preliminary notice on the freeholder. This has the same function as with collective enfranchisement: it commits the leaseholder to nothing, but requires the freeholder to supply within 28 days the information that will enable the leaseholder to decide whether to go ahead.

The procedure is modelled on that for collective enfranchisement:

- The leaseholder serves an initial notice (a 'section 42 notice') on the freeholder. This must give details of the property concerned as well as of the leaseholder and his claim to qualify to use the 1993 Act. It must state how much the leaseholder proposes to pay, and set a date, at least two months ahead, by which the freeholder must reply. Once the notice has been served, the leaseholder must allow the freeholder to have access to the flat for the purpose of valuation.

- The freeholder must either agree that the leaseholder qualifies under the Act, or give reasons for disagreeing. If the freeholder agrees that the leaseholder is qualified to extend the lease, he may still suggest a that price of the new lease, or its other terms, should be different to the leaseholder's proposals. The freeholder can go to court for permission to reject the extension entirely if the current lease has less than five years to run and the freeholder then intends to redevelop the property.

- The freeholder and leaseholder should then attempt to resolve any differences by negotiation. If agreement is not reached, the question may be referred to the leasehold valuation tribunal at lease two months, and not less than six months, after the freeholder's counter notice. If, six months after the counter notice, there is neither an agreement nor a referral to a tribunal, the leaseholder's initial notice will be deemed withdrawn. In this event the leaseholder is liable for any reasonable expenses incurred by the freeholder.

- Once the terms are settled, either by negotiation or by the tribunal, the parties have two months to exchange contracts. If exchange does not take place during this period, the leaseholder has a further two months to apply to court for an order extending the lease on the terms agreed (or laid down by a tribunal).

It should be noted that collective enfranchisement takes priority over individual lease extensions, so that the effect of an initial notice of collective enfranchisement is to freeze, for the time being, any current claims to extend leases. If the collective enfranchisement fails to go ahead, the extension claims resume where they left off.

INDEX

Agricultural holdings, 18
Agricultural Holdings Act of 1986, 52
Agricultural tenancies, 52
Agricultural worker condition, 65
Alterations, 26
Arbitration, 100
Assigning a secure tenancy, 25
Assignment of Leases, 106
Assignment through succession, 25
Assignment to a potential successor, 25
Assured Agricultural occupancies, 64
Assured shorthold tenancy, 6
Common Parts Assistance, 82
Common Parts Loan, 82
Commonhold, 72, 84, 88, 91, 100, 111, 113, 122, 125, 126
Commonhold and Leasehold Reform Act 2002, 84, 88, 91, 125, 126
Company lets, 19
Compensation for improvements, 58
Conditions of tenancy, 7
Council tax, 7, 70, 71
Council tax benefits available for those on low income, 71
Criminal Law Act 1977, 10

Crown Estate Commissioners, 42
Damages, 76, 78
Decent Homes Loans Assistance, 82
Deposits, 73
Different types of tenancy agreement, 9
Disabled Facilities Assistance, 82
Disabled Facilities Grant, 81
Disabled tenants, 80
Discretionary grounds for possession, 13
Ending a tenancy, 7
Energy Innovation Grants, 83
Enfranchisement, 124, 125, 133
Excluded properties from the right to buy, 31
Exclusive possession, 100
Extension of a Lease, 125
Farm business tenancy, 52
Fast track possession, 47
Fixed term tenancy, 6
Flats and houses let with other land, 17
Forfeiture, 107, 108, 121
freehold, 5, 30, 31, 33, 84, 85, 87, 88, 89, 90, 92, 111, 115, 124, 125, 128, 129, 130, 131, 132, 133, 134, 135, 136, 137, 138, 139
Grounds for possession, 8, 12, 34

Head leases, 90
Holiday lettings, 18
Hostels, 81
Houses in Multiple
   Occupation, 80
Housing Act 2004, 80
Housing Action Trust, 21, 43
Housing benefit, 68
Housing Grants, 81
Injunction, 75
Introductory tenancies, 22, 23
Joint tenancies, 48
Land acquired for
   development, 23
Landlords consent for
   planning permission, 58
Landlords Major Works
   Assistance, 82
Landlords obligations, 7
Law of Property Act 1925,
   108
lease, 5, 30, 31, 53, 85, 86, 87,
   88, 89, 90, 92, 93, 94, 95,
   96, 97, 99, 100, 101, 102,
   104, 106, 107, 108, 110,
   111, 113, 115, 116, 117,
   120, 121, 122, 123, 124,
   125, 126, 127, 128, 129,
   132, 136, 137, 138, 139,
   140
Leasehold Reform Act 1967,
   88, 124, 127
Leasehold Reform Housing
   and Urban Development
   Act 1993, 27
Leasehold Reform, Housing
   and Urban Development

Act 1993, 88, 103, 106,
   124, 128, 133
Leasehold Valuation Tribunal,
   93, 100, 104, 106, 113, 115,
   117, 118, 120, 122, 133
Leaseholders' Right to
   Manage, 103
Lettings to students, 18
Licensed premises, 18
Licensee, 10
Mandatory grounds for
   possession, 12
Matrimonial proceedings, 25
Minor work assistance, 83
Mobile home, 49
Mutual exchange, 25
Notice to quit, 12
Overcrowding, 8, 37
Payment of rent, 47
Payments for board and
   attendance, 18
Periodic tenancies, 28
Periodic tenancy, 6
Powers of Leaseholders over
   Management, 103
Procedure for the right to
   buy, 32
Protected occupier, 61
Protection from Eviction Act
   1977, 10, 12, 74
Protection of Residential
   Agricultural workers, 59
Recognised Tenants'
   Association, 106
Reductions in council tax
   bills, 71